W9-APT-507

FAVORITE BRAND NAME™

Silly Snacks

pil

Publications International, Ltd.

Favorite Brand Name Recipes at www.fbnr.com

Copyright © 2004 Publications International, Ltd.
All rights reserved. This publication may not be reproduced or quoted in whole
or in part by any means whatsoever without written permission from:

Louis Weber, CEO
Publications International, Ltd.
7373 North Cicero Avenue
Lincolnwood, IL 60712

Permission is never granted for commercial purposes.

Favorite Brand Name is a trademark of Publications International, Ltd.

All recipes and photographs that contain specific brand names are copyrighted
by those companies and/or associations, unless otherwise specified. All
photographs copyright © Publications International, Ltd.

DOLE® is a registered trademark of Dole Food Company, Inc.

™/© M&M's, M and the M&M's Characters are trademarks of
Mars, Incorporated.
© Mars, Inc. 2004.

Some of the products listed in this publication may be in limited distribution.

Pictured on the front cover: Mice Creams *(page 210).*
Pictured on the back cover *(clockwise from top left):* Little Piggy Pie
(page 104), Cool Sandwich Snacks *(page 42)* and Dino-Mite Dinosaurs
(page 8).

ISBN-13: 978-0-7853-9677-2
ISBN-10: 0-7853-9677-2

Library of Congress Control Number: 2003109983

Manufactured in China.

8 7 6 5 4 3 2 1

Microwave Cooking: Microwave ovens vary in wattage. Use the cooking times
as guidelines and check for doneness before adding more time.

Preparation/Cooking Times: Preparation times are based on the approximate
amount of time required to assemble the recipe before cooking, baking, chilling
or serving. These times include preparation steps such as measuring, chopping
and mixing. The fact that some preparations and cooking can be done
simultaneously is taken into account. Preparation of optional ingredients and
serving suggestions is not included.

Table of Contents

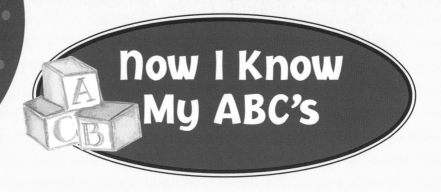

Apple Oatmeal Snack Bars

1½ cups all-purpose flour

¾ cup uncooked rolled oats

1 teaspoon baking powder

½ teaspoon salt

1 cup granulated sugar

2 tablespoons margarine, softened

½ cup MOTT'S® Cinnamon Apple Sauce

1 egg

1 teaspoon vanilla extract

1 cup MOTT'S® Chunky Apple Sauce

⅓ cup raisins

1 tablespoon firmly packed light brown sugar

½ teaspoon ground cinnamon

1. Preheat oven to 375°F. Spray 8-inch square baking pan with nonstick cooking spray.

2. In medium bowl, combine flour, oats, baking powder and salt.

3. In large bowl, beat granulated sugar and margarine with electric mixer at medium speed until blended. Whisk in ½ cup cinnamon apple sauce, egg and vanilla. Add flour mixture to apple sauce mixture; stir until well blended. Spoon half of batter into prepared pan, spreading evenly.

4. In small bowl, combine 1 cup chunky apple sauce, raisins, brown sugar and cinnamon. Pour evenly over batter. Spoon remaining batter over filling, spreading evenly.

5. Bake 30 to 35 minutes or until lightly browned. Cool on wire rack 15 minutes; cut into 16 bars.   *Makes 16 servings*

Bagelroonies

6 onion bagels
6 tablespoons soft-spread margarine
1 (14-ounce) jar NEWMAN'S OWN® Sockarooni™ Sauce
1 (8-ounce) package Canadian bacon slices
1 (16-ounce) package mozzarella cheese, shredded (2 cups)
Freshly grated Parmesan cheese

Cut bagels in half; spread with margarine. Spoon Newman's Own®
Sockarooni sauce on bagel halves, approximately 3 tablespoons per bagel
half. Chop Canadian bacon slices and place over sauce. Sprinkle liberally
with shredded mozzarella cheese. If desired, shake grated Parmesan
cheese over bagels. Broil until cheese melts and bubbles.

Makes 6 servings

Super Suggestion!

**Sliced mushrooms, green olives, black
olives or jalapeños may be sprinkled
over mozzarella cheese.**

Cereal Trail Mix

¼ cup butter or margarine

2 tablespoons sugar

1 teaspoon ground cinnamon

1 cup bite-sized oat cereal squares

1 cup bite-sized wheat cereal squares

1 cup bite-sized rice cereal squares

¼ cup toasted slivered almonds

¾ cup raisins

1. Melt butter at HIGH (100%) 1½ minutes in large microwave-safe bowl. Add sugar and cinnamon; mix well. Add cereals and almonds; stir to coat.

2. Microwave at HIGH 2 minutes. Stir well. Microwave 2 minutes more; stir well. Add raisins. Microwave an additional 2 to 3 minutes, stirring well after 2 minutes. Spread on paper towels; mix will become crisp as it cools. Store tightly covered.   *Makes about 4 cups*

● ● ● ● ● ● ● ● ● ● ●

**Why did the boy throw
butter out the window?**

● ● ● ● ● ● ● ● ● ● ●

Answer: Because he wanted to see a butterfly.

Dino-Mite Dinosaurs

1 cup (2 sticks) butter, softened
1¼ cups granulated sugar
1 large egg
2 squares (1 ounce each) semi-sweet chocolate, melted
½ teaspoon vanilla extract
2⅓ cups all-purpose flour
1 teaspoon baking powder
¼ teaspoon salt
1 cup white frosting
Assorted food colorings
1 cup "M&M's"® Chocolate Mini Baking Bits

In large bowl cream butter and sugar until light and fluffy; beat in egg, chocolate and vanilla. In medium bowl combine flour, baking powder and salt; add to creamed mixture; mix well. Wrap and refrigerate dough 2 to 3 hours. Preheat oven to 350°F. Working with half the dough at a time on lightly floured surface, roll to ¼-inch thickness. Cut into dinosaur shapes using 4-inch cookie cutters. Place about 2 inches apart on ungreased cookie sheets. Bake 10 to 12 minutes. Cool 2 minutes on cookie sheets; cool completely on wire racks. Tint frosting desired colors. Frost cookies and decorate with "M&M's"® Chocolate Mini Baking Bits. Store in tightly covered container.   *Makes 2 dozen cookies*

Easy Nachos

> 4 (6-inch) flour tortillas
> Nonstick cooking spray
> 4 ounces ground turkey
> ⅔ cup salsa (mild or medium)
> 2 tablespoons sliced green onion
> ½ cup (2 ounces) shredded reduced-fat Cheddar cheese

1. Preheat oven to 350°F. Cut each tortilla into 8 wedges; lightly spray one side of wedges with cooking spray. Place on ungreased baking sheet. Bake 5 to 9 minutes or until lightly browned and crisp.

2. Cook ground turkey in small nonstick skillet until browned, stirring with spoon to break up meat. Drain fat. Stir in salsa. Cook until hot.

3. Sprinkle meat mixture over tortilla wedges. Sprinkle with green onion. Top with cheese. Return to oven 1 to 2 minutes or until cheese melts.   *Makes 4 servings*

Serving Suggestion: Cut tortillas into shapes with cookie cutters and bake as directed.

Note: In a hurry? Substitute baked corn chips for flour tortillas and cooking spray. Proceed as directed.

Firecrackers

5 cups BAKER'S® ANGEL FLAKE® Coconut
   Red food coloring
24 baked cupcakes, cooled
  1 tub (12 ounces) COOL WHIP® Whipped Topping, thawed
   Blue decorating gel
   Red string licorice

TINT coconut using red food coloring.

TRIM any "lips" off top edges of cupcakes. Using small amount of whipped topping, attach bottoms of 2 cupcakes together. Repeat with remaining cupcakes. Stand attached cupcakes on 1 end on serving plate or tray.

FROST with remaining whipped topping. Press coconut onto sides.

DRAW a star on top of each firecracker with decorating gel. Insert pieces of licorice for fuses. Store cakes in refrigerator.

Makes 12 Firecrackers

Grilled Cheese & Turkey Shapes

8 slices seedless rye or sourdough bread

8 teaspoons *French's*® Mustard, any flavor

8 slices deli roast turkey

4 slices American cheese

2 tablespoons butter or margarine, softened

1. Spread *1 teaspoon* mustard on each slice of bread. Arrange turkey and cheese on half of the bread slices, dividing evenly. Cover with top halves of bread.

2. Cut out sandwich shapes using choice of cookie cutters. Place cookie cutter on top of sandwich; press down firmly. Remove excess trimmings.

3. Spread butter on both sides of sandwich. Heat large nonstick skillet over medium heat. Cook sandwiches 1 minute per side or until bread is golden and cheese melts.   *Makes 4 sandwiches*

Tip: Use 2½-inch star, heart, teddy bear or flower-shaped cookie cutters.

Prep Time: 15 minutes
Cook Time: 2 minutes

• • • • • • • • • • • •

What does a turkey like to eat on Thanksgiving?

• • • • • • • • • • • •

Answer: Nothing. He is already stuffed.

Handprints

1 package (20 ounces) refrigerated cookie dough, any flavor
All-purpose flour (optional)
Cookie glazes, frostings and assorted candies

1. Grease cookie sheets. Remove dough from wrapper according to package directions.

2. Cut dough into 4 equal sections. Reserve 1 section; refrigerate remaining 3 sections. Sprinkle reserved dough with flour to minimize sticking, if necessary.

3. Roll dough on prepared cookie sheet to 5×7-inch rectangle.

4. Place hand, palm-side down, on dough. Carefully, cut around outline of hand with knife. Remove scraps. Separate fingers as much as possible using small spatula. Pat fingers outward to lengthen slightly. Repeat steps with remaining dough.

5. Freeze dough 15 minutes. Preheat oven to 350°F.

6. Bake 7 to 13 minutes or until cookies are set and edges are golden brown. Cool completely on cookie sheets.

7. Decorate as desired. *Makes 5 adult handprint cookies*

Tip: To get the kids involved, let them use their hands to make the handprints. Be sure that an adult is available to cut around the outline with a knife. The kids will enjoy seeing how their handprints bake into big cookies.

Instant Individual Pizza

1 6-inch whole-wheat tortilla

1 tablespoon no salt added tomato sauce *or* 2 teaspoons basil pesto sauce

¼ teaspoon dried oregano

2 tablespoons shredded reduced-fat Swiss or part-skim mozzarella cheese

1. Preheat oven to 500°F.

2. Spread tortilla to edges with tomato sauce or basil pesto sauce. Sprinkle with oregano. Top with cheese.

3. Place on pizza pan or baking sheet and bake about 5 minutes or until tortilla is crisp and cheese is bubbly. *Makes 1 serving*

Jammy Pinwheels

1¼ cups granulated sugar

1 Butter Flavor **CRISCO®** Stick or 1 cup Butter Flavor **CRISCO®** all-vegetable shortening plus additional for greasing

2 eggs

¼ cup light corn syrup or regular pancake syrup

1 tablespoon vanilla

3 cups all-purpose flour plus 2 tablespoons, divided

¾ teaspoon baking powder

½ teaspoon baking soda

½ teaspoon salt

1 cup **SMUCKER'S®** Apricot, Strawberry or Seedless Raspberry Jam

1. Place sugar and 1 cup shortening in large bowl. Beat at medium speed of electric mixer until well blended. Add eggs, syrup and vanilla; beat until well blended and fluffy.

2. Combine 3 cups flour, baking powder, baking soda and salt. Add gradually to shortening mixture, beating at low speed until well blended.

3. Divide dough in half. Pat each half into thick rectangle. Sprinkle about 1 tablespoon flour on large sheet of waxed paper. Place rectangle of dough on floured paper. Turn dough over; cover with another large sheet of waxed paper. Roll dough into an 12×8-inch rectangle about ⅛ inch thick. Trim edges. Slide dough and waxed paper onto ungreased baking sheets. Refrigerate 20 minutes or until firm. Repeat with remaining dough.

4. Heat oven to 375°F. Grease baking sheets. Place sheets of foil on counter for cooling cookies.

5. Place chilled dough rectangle on work surface. Remove top sheet of waxed paper. Cut dough into 2-inch squares. Place squares 2 inches apart on prepared baking sheets. Make a 1-inch diagonal cut from each corner of square almost to center. Place 1 teaspoon jam in center. Lift every other corner and bring together in center of cookie. Repeat with remaining dough.

6. Bake at 375°F for 7 to 10 minutes or until edges of cookies are golden brown. *Do not overbake.* Cool 2 minutes on baking sheet. Remove cookies to foil to cool completely.   *Makes about 4 dozen cookies*

Super Suggestion!

Most cookies bake quickly and should be watched carefully to avoid overbaking. Check them at the minimum baking time, then watch carefully to make sure they don't burn. It is generally better to slightly underbake rather than to overbake cookies.

Kaleidoscope Honey Pops

2¼ cups water

¾ cup honey

3 cups assorted fruit, cut into small pieces

12 (3-ounce) paper cups or popsicle molds

12 popsicle sticks

Whisk together water and honey in pitcher until well blended. Place ¼ cup fruit in each mold. Divide honey mixture between cups. Freeze about 1 hour or until partially frozen. Insert popsicle sticks; freeze until firm and ready to serve.   *Makes 12 servings*

Favorite recipe from **National Honey Board**

Leapin' Lizards!

1 cup butterscotch-flavor chips

½ cup corn syrup

3 tablespoons butter

1 cup white chocolate chips

Green food color

7 cups crisp rice cereal

Candy corn, green jelly beans, red miniature jaw breakers and chocolate chips

1. Line baking sheet with waxed paper.

2. Combine butterscotch chips, corn syrup and butter in large saucepan. Stir over medium heat until chips are melted. Add white chocolate chips and green food color; stir well. Remove from heat. Add cereal; stir to coat evenly.

3. Lightly butter hands and shape about 1½ cups cereal mixture into lizard (about 6 inches long) as shown in photo. Place on prepared baking sheet. Decorate with candies as shown. Repeat with remaining mixture.

Makes 4 lizards

20

From top to bottom: Magic Wands (page 185), Leapin' Lizards!

Make Your Own Pizza Shapes

1 package (10 ounces) refrigerated pizza dough
¼ to ½ cup prepared pizza sauce
1 cup shredded mozzarella cheese
1 cup *French's*® French Fried Onions

1. Preheat oven to 425°F. Unroll dough onto greased baking sheet. Press or roll dough into 12×8-inch rectangle. With sharp knife or pizza cutter, cut dough into large shape of your choice (butterfly, heart, star). Reroll scraps and cut into mini shapes. (See tip.)

2. Pre-bake crust 7 minutes or until crust just begins to brown. Spread with sauce and top with cheese. Bake 6 minutes or until crust is deep golden brown.

3. Sprinkle with French Fried Onions. Bake 2 minutes longer or until golden. *Makes 4 to 6 servings*

Tip: Pizza dough can be cut with 6-inch shaped cookie cutters. Spread with sauce and top with cheese. Bake about 10 minutes or until crust is golden. Sprinkle with French Fried Onions. Bake 2 minutes longer.

Prep Time: 10 minutes
Cook Time: 15 minutes

No-Bake Banana Peanut Butter Fudge Bars

1 ripe, large **DOLE®** Banana
⅔ cup butter or margarine
2 teaspoons vanilla extract
2½ cups rolled oats
½ cup packed brown sugar
1 cup semisweet chocolate chips
½ cup peanut butter

• Finely chop banana (1¼ cups). Melt butter in large skillet over medium heat; stir in vanilla. Add oats and brown sugar. Heat and stir 5 minutes. Set aside ¾ cup oat mixture. Press remaining oat mixture into greased 9-inch square baking pan. Sprinkle banana over crust.

• Melt chocolate chips and peanut butter together over low heat. Pour and spread over banana. Sprinkle with reserved oat mixture; press down lightly. Chill 2 hours before cutting. Store in refrigerator.

Makes 24 bars

Octo-Dogs and Shells

4 hot dogs
1½ cups uncooked small shell pasta
1½ cups frozen mixed vegetables
1 cup prepared Alfredo sauce
Prepared yellow mustard in squeeze bottle
Cheese-flavored fish-shaped crackers

Lay 1 hot dog on side with end facing you. Starting 1 inch from one end of hot dog, slice hot dog vertically in half. Roll hot dog ¼ turn and slice in half vertically again, making 4 segments connected at the top. Slice each segment in half vertically, creating a total of 8 "legs." Repeat with remaining hot dogs.

Place hot dogs in medium saucepan; cover with water. Bring to a boil over medium-high heat. Remove from heat; set aside.

Prepare pasta according to package directions, stirring in vegetables during last 3 minutes of cooking time. Drain; return to pan. Stir in Alfredo sauce. Heat over low heat until heated through. Divide pasta mixture between four plates.

Drain octo-dogs. Arrange one octo-dog on top of pasta mixture on each plate. Draw faces on "heads" of octo-dogs with mustard. Sprinkle crackers over pasta mixture.   *Makes 4 servings*

Piggy Wraps

1 package **HILLSHIRE FARM®** Lit'l Smokies
2 cans (8 ounces each) refrigerated crescent roll dough, cut
   into small triangles

Preheat oven to 400°F.

Wrap individual Lit'l Smokies in dough triangles. Bake 5 minutes or until
golden brown.   *Makes about 50 hors d'oeuvres*

Note: Piggy Wraps may be frozen. To reheat in microwave, microwave at
HIGH 1½ minutes or at MEDIUM-HIGH (70% power) 2 minutes. When
reheated in microwave, dough will not be crisp.

Quick Pizza Snacks

3 English muffins, split and toasted
1 can (14½ ounces) Italian-style diced tomatoes, undrained
¾ cup (3 ounces) shredded Italian cheese blend
   Bell pepper strips (optional)

Preheat oven to 350°F. Place English muffin halves on ungreased baking
sheet. Top each muffin with ¼ cup tomatoes; sprinkle with 2 tablespoons
cheese. Bake about 5 minutes or until cheese is melted and lightly
browned. Garnish with bell pepper strips, if desired.
                                             Makes 6 servings

Reese's® Haystacks

1⅔ cups (10-ounce package) REESE'S® Peanut Butter Chips

1 tablespoon shortening (do *not* use butter, margarine, spread or oil)

2½ cups (5-ounce can) chow mein noodles

1. Line tray with wax paper.

2. Place peanut butter chips and shortening in medium microwave-safe bowl. Microwave at HIGH (100%) 1 minute; stir. If necessary, microwave at HIGH an additional 15 seconds at a time, stirring after each heating, just until chips are melted and mixture is smooth when stirred. Immediately add chow mein noodles; stir to coat.

3. Drop mixture by heaping teaspoons onto prepared tray or into paper candy cups. Let stand until firm. If necessary, cover and refrigerate several minutes until firm. Store in tightly covered container.

Makes about 2 dozen treats

● ● ● ● ● ● ● ● ● ● ● ● ●

Why did the cookie go to the doctor's office?

● ● ● ● ● ● ● ● ● ● ● ● ●

Answer: Because he was feeling crummy!

Savory Zucchini Stix

Nonstick olive oil cooking spray

3 tablespoons seasoned dry bread crumbs

2 tablespoons grated Parmesan cheese

I egg white

I teaspoon reduced-fat (2%) milk

2 small zucchini (about 4 ounces each), cut lengthwise into quarters

⅓ cup spaghetti sauce, warmed

1. Preheat oven to 400°F. Spray baking sheet with cooking spray; set aside.

2. Combine bread crumbs and Parmesan cheese in shallow dish. Combine egg white and milk in another shallow dish; beat with fork until well blended.

3. Dip each zucchini wedge first into crumb mixture, then into egg white mixture, letting excess drip back into dish. Roll again in crumb mixture to coat.

4. Place zucchini quarters on prepared baking sheet; coat well with cooking spray. Bake 15 to 18 minutes or until golden brown. Serve with spaghetti sauce. *Makes 4 servings*

Tic-Tac-Toe Tuna Pizza

- 1 bread-style prepared pizza crust (10 ounces)
- 1 can (12 ounces) tuna packed in water, drained
- ½ cup minced onion
- ⅓ cup reduced-fat mayonnaise
- 9 thin plum tomato slices
- 4 to 5 slices (¾ ounce each) process cheese food or American cheese

1. Preheat oven to 425°F. Place bread shell on pizza pan or baking sheet.

2. Combine tuna, onion and mayonnaise in medium bowl; season to taste with salt and pepper. Stir until blended. Spread mixture over bread shell, leaving 1-inch border. Arrange tomato slices on tuna mixture in 3 rows, spacing at least ½ inch apart.

3. Bake 10 to 12 minutes or until heated through.

4. While pizza is baking, cut cheese slices into ½-inch-wide strips.

5. Remove pizza from oven. Arrange enough strips over tuna mixture to resemble tic-tac-toe game. Crisscross remaining strips over some tomato slices. Let stand 5 minutes before serving.   *Makes 6 servings*

Prep and Cook Time: 30 minutes

Uncle Sam's Hat

1 package (about 18 ounces) refrigerated chocolate chip
     cookie dough
2 cups powdered sugar
2 to 4 tablespoons milk
   Red and blue food colors

1. Preheat oven to 350°F. Lightly grease 12-inch round pizza pan and baking sheet. Remove dough from wrapper. Press dough evenly into prepared pizza pan. Cut dough into hat shape. Using 1½- to 2-inch star cookie cutter, cut out several stars; remove and discard dough scraps. Place stars on baking sheet.

2. Bake stars 5 to 7 minutes and hat 7 to 9 minutes or until lightly browned at edges. Cool stars on baking sheet 1 minute. Remove stars to wire rack; cool completely. Cool hat completely in pan on rack.

3. Combine powdered sugar and enough milk, one tablespoon at a time, to make medium-thick pourable glaze. Spread small amount of glaze over stars and place on waxed paper; let stand until glaze is set. Using red and blue food colors, tint ½ of glaze red, tint ¼ of glaze blue and leave remaining ¼ of glaze white.

4. Decorate hat with red, white and blue glazes; place stars on hat. Let stand until glaze is set.   *Makes 1 large cookie*

Vegetable Martians

10 cherry tomatoes, baby pattypan squash or combination
 5 to 10 thin slices cucumber or zucchini
¼ teaspoon reduced-fat soft cream cheese or mustard
 5 to 8 currants, cut into halves
10 chow mein noodles

Skewer vegetables on wooden picks to form martian bodies. Use cream cheese or mustard to make eyes or to attach currants for eyes and mouths. Press 2 chow mein noodles into top of each martian for antennae. Remove wooden picks before serving.   *Makes 5 martians*

Wormy Apples

6 medium apples, such as Jonathan or Pink Lady

½ cup maple syrup

⅓ cup water

1 teaspoon lemon juice

2 (1-inch) strips lemon peel

¼ teaspoon ground cinnamon

   Dash salt

2 tablespoons butter

6 to 12 soft candy worms

1. Preheat oven to 350°F. Core apples, being careful not to cut through to bottom. Peel top ⅓ of apple. Stand apples in baking pan.

2. Combine maple syrup, water, lemon juice, lemon peel, cinnamon and salt in small saucepan. Bring to a boil. Pour mixture over apples. Cover loosely with foil.

3. Bake 30 minutes. Remove from oven. Place 1 teaspoon butter into core of each apple. Baste apples with pan juices; cover and bake 15 minutes or until tender. Cool.

4. Cut 1 or 2 small holes from outside of apple through to the core. Thread worms halfway through the holes. Serve warm or cold.

Makes 6 servings

Super Suggestion!

Apples will keep in a cool, dry place for a week or two. For longer storage, place apples in a plastic bag and store in the refrigerator. Apples in good condition can last up to six weeks in the refrigerator.

Xippy Cookie Pops

I package (20 ounces) refrigerated sugar cookie dough
All-purpose flour (optional)
20 (4-inch) lollipop sticks
Assorted frostings, glazes and decors

1. Preheat oven to 350°F. Grease cookie sheets.

2. Remove dough from wrapper according to package directions. Sprinkle with flour to minimize sticking, if necessary.

3. Cut dough in half. Reserve I half; refrigerate remaining dough. Roll reserved dough to 1/8-inch thickness. Cut out cookies using 3½-inch cookie cutters.

4. Place lollipop sticks on cookies so that tips of sticks are imbedded in cookies. Carefully turn cookies so sticks are in back; place on prepared cookie sheets. Repeat with remaining dough.

5. Bake 7 to 11 minutes or until edges are lightly browned. Cool cookies on cookie sheets 2 minutes. Remove cookies to wire racks; cool completely.

6. Decorate with frostings, glazes and decors as desired.

Makes 20 cookies

Yummy Frozen Chocolate-Covered Bananas

2 ripe medium bananas
4 wooden sticks
½ cup low-fat granola cereal without raisins
⅓ cup hot fudge sauce, at room temperature

1. Line baking sheet or 15×10-inch jelly-roll pan with waxed paper; set aside.

2. Peel bananas; cut each in half crosswise. Insert wooden stick into center of cut end of each banana about 1½ inches into banana half. Place on prepared baking sheet; freeze until firm, at least 2 hours.

3. Place granola in large plastic food storage bag; crush slightly using rolling pin or meat mallet. Transfer granola to shallow plate. Place fudge sauce in shallow dish.

4. Working with 1 banana at a time, place frozen banana in fudge sauce; turn banana and spread fudge sauce evenly onto banana with small rubber scraper. Immediately place banana on plate with granola; turn to coat lightly. Return to baking sheet in freezer. Repeat with remaining bananas.

5. Freeze until fudge sauce is very firm, at least 2 hours. Place on small plates; let stand 5 minutes before serving.   *Makes 4 servings*

● ● ● ● ● ● ● ● ● ● ● ●

What is the difference between a fish and a piano?

● ● ● ● ● ● ● ● ● ● ● ●

Answer: You can't tuna fish!

Zippity Hot Doggity Tacos

1 small onion, finely chopped

1 tablespoon *Frank's® RedHot®* Cayenne Pepper Sauce or *French's®* Worcestershire Sauce

4 frankfurters, chopped

1 can (10½ ounces) red kidney or black beans, drained

1 can (8 ounces) tomato sauce

1 teaspoon chili powder

8 taco shells, heated

1 cup *French's®* French Fried Onions

Garnish: chopped tomatoes, shredded lettuce, sliced olives, sour cream, shredded cheese

1. Heat *1 tablespoon oil* in 12-inch nonstick skillet over medium-high heat. Cook onion, 3 minutes or until crisp-tender. Stir in next five ingredients through chili powder. Bring to boiling. Reduce heat to medium-low and cook 5 minutes, stirring occasionally.

2. To serve, spoon chili into taco shells. Garnish as desired and sprinkle with French Fried Onions. Splash on **Frank's RedHot** Sauce for extra zip! *Makes 4 servings*

Prep Time: 5 minutes
Cook Time: 8 minutes

Snacks on the Go

Cool Sandwich Snacks

10 whole graham crackers or chocolate-flavor graham
    crackers, cracked in half

½ cup chocolate fudge sauce

1 tub (8 ounces) COOL WHIP® Whipped Topping, thawed

    Suggested Garnishes: Multi-colored sprinkles, assorted
    candies, finely crushed cookies, chocolate chunks,
    chopped nuts or toasted BAKER'S® ANGEL FLAKE®
    Coconut

SPREAD ½ of the graham crackers lightly with chocolate sauce. Spread whipped topping about ¾ inch thick on remaining ½ of the graham crackers. Press crackers together lightly, making sandwiches. Roll or lightly press edges in suggested garnishes.

FREEZE 4 hours or overnight.   *Makes 10 sandwiches*

Make Ahead: This recipe can be made up to 2 weeks ahead. Wrap well with plastic wrap and freeze.

Prep Time: 15 minutes
Freeze Time: 4 hours

• • • • • • • • • • • •

How do you make a strawberry shake?

• • • • • • • • • • • •

Answer: Take it to a scary movie!

Cinnamon Trail Mix

2 cups corn cereal squares

2 cups whole wheat cereal squares or whole wheat cereal squares with mini graham crackers

1½ cups fat-free oyster crackers

½ cup broken sesame snack sticks

2 tablespoons margarine or butter, melted

1 teaspoon ground cinnamon

¼ teaspoon ground nutmeg

½ cup bite-sized fruit-flavored candy pieces

1. Preheat oven to 350°F. Spray 13×9-inch baking pan with nonstick cooking spray.

2. Place cereals, oyster crackers and sesame sticks in prepared pan; mix lightly.

3. Combine margarine, cinnamon and nutmeg in small bowl; mix well. Drizzle evenly over cereal mixture; toss to coat.

4. Bake 12 to 14 minutes or until golden brown, stirring gently after 6 minutes. Cool completely. Stir in candies.   *Makes 8 (¾-cup) servings*

Super Suggestion!

Store leftover trail mix in a tightly sealed container or a resealable plastic food storage bag.

Funny Face Sandwich Melts

2 super-size English muffins, split and toasted
8 teaspoons *French's*® Sweet & Tangy Honey Mustard
1 can (8 ounces) crushed pineapple, drained
8 ounces sliced smoked ham
4 slices Swiss cheese or white American cheese

1. Place English muffins, cut side up, on baking sheet. Spread each with 2 *teaspoons* mustard. Arrange one-fourth of the pineapple, ham and cheese on top, dividing evenly.

2. Broil until cheese melts, about 1 minute. Decorate with mustard and assorted vegetables to create your own funny face.   *Makes 4 servings*

Tip: This sandwich is also easy to prepare in the toaster oven.

Prep Time: 10 minutes
Cook Time: 1 minute

Sugar-and-Spice Twists

1 tablespoon sugar
¼ teaspoon ground cinnamon
1 package (6) refrigerated breadsticks

1. Preheat oven to 350°F. Lightly grease baking sheet or line with parchment paper.

2. Combine sugar and cinnamon in shallow dish or plate.

3. Open package of breadsticks. Divide into 6 portions. Roll each portion into 12-inch rope. Roll in sugar mixture. Twist into pretzel shape. Place on prepared baking sheet. Bake 15 to 18 minutes or until lightly browned. Remove from baking sheet. Cool 5 minutes. Serve warm.
Makes 6 servings

Tip: Use colored sugar sprinkles in place of the sugar in this recipe for a fun 'twist' of color that's perfect for holidays, birthdays or simply everyday celebrations.

Funny Face Sandwich Melt

Hot Dog Burritos

1 can (16 ounces) pork and beans
⅓ cup ketchup
2 tablespoons *French's®* Classic Yellow® Mustard
2 tablespoons brown sugar
8 frankfurters, cooked
8 (8-inch) flour tortillas, heated

1. Combine beans, ketchup, mustard and brown sugar in medium saucepan. Bring to boiling over medium-high heat. Reduce heat to low and simmer 2 minutes.

2. Arrange frankfurters in heated tortillas and top with bean mixture. Roll up jelly-roll style.   *Makes 8 servings*

Tip: Try topping dogs with *French's®* French Fried Onions before rolling up!

Prep Time: 5 minutes
Cook Time: 8 minutes

Kool-Pop Treat

1 (3-ounce) bag ORVILLE REDENBACHER'S® Microwave Popping Corn, popped according to package directions
2 cups brightly colored puffed oat cereal, such as fruit flavored loops
2 cups miniature marshmallows
1 (.35-ounce) package strawberry soft drink mix
2 tablespoons powdered sugar

1. In large bowl, combine popcorn, cereal and marshmallows.

2. Combine drink mix and powdered sugar; sift over popcorn mixture. Toss to coat.   *Makes 12 (1-cup) servings*

Bread Pudding Snacks

1¼ cups reduced-fat (2%) milk

½ cup cholesterol-free egg substitute

⅓ cup sugar

1 teaspoon vanilla

⅛ teaspoon salt

⅛ teaspoon ground nutmeg (optional)

4 cups ½-inch cinnamon or cinnamon-raisin bread cubes (about 6 bread slices)

1 tablespoon margarine or butter, melted

1. Combine milk, egg substitute, sugar, vanilla, salt and nutmeg, if desired, in medium bowl; mix well. Add bread; mix until well moistened. Let stand at room temperature 15 minutes.

2. Preheat oven to 350°F. Line 12 medium-size muffin cups with paper liners.

3. Spoon bread mixture evenly into prepared cups; drizzle evenly with margarine.

4. Bake 30 to 35 minutes or until snacks are puffed and golden brown. Remove to wire rack to cool completely.   *Makes 12 servings*

Note: Snacks will puff up in the oven and fall slightly upon cooling.

Teddy Bear Party Mix

4 cups crisp cinnamon graham cereal

2 cups honey flavored teddy-shaped graham snacks

1 can (1½ ounces) *French's*® Potato Sticks

3 tablespoons melted unsalted butter

2 tablespoons *French's*® Worcestershire Sauce

1 tablespoon packed brown sugar

¼ teaspoon ground cinnamon

1 cup sweetened dried cranberries or raisins

½ cup chocolate, peanut butter or carob chips

1. Preheat oven to 350°F. Lightly spray jelly-roll pan with nonstick cooking spray. Combine cereal, graham snacks and potato sticks in large bowl.

2. Combine butter, Worcestershire, sugar and cinnamon in small bowl; toss with cereal mixture. Transfer to prepared pan. Bake 12 minutes. Cool completely.

3. Stir in dried cranberries and chips. Store in an air-tight container.

Makes about 7 cups

Prep Time: 5 minutes
Cook Time: 12 minutes

● ● ● ● ● ● ● ● ● ● ● ●

**Where is the best place to
see a man-eating fish?**

● ● ● ● ● ● ● ● ● ● ● ●

Answer: In a seafood restaurant!

Easy Cinnamon-Raisin Snails

Snails

> 2 to 3 tablespoons flour
>
> 1 loaf (16 ounces) frozen bread dough, completely thawed
>
> 3 tablespoons butter or margarine, divided
>
> ½ cup packed brown sugar
>
> 2 teaspoons cinnamon
>
> ¾ cup **SUN-MAID®** Raisins or Golden Raisins

Glaze

> ¼ cup powdered sugar
>
> 1 to 2 teaspoons milk

1. **LINE** a baking sheet with aluminum foil for easy clean-up.

2. **SPRINKLE** flour on counter or a large cutting board. Roll dough with a rolling pin on floured surface to an 18×8-inch rectangle.

3. **MELT*** 2 tablespoons butter in a microwave-safe bowl on HIGH for 1 minute. Stir in brown sugar, cinnamon and raisins; sprinkle evenly over dough except on 1 inch along one long side.

4. **ROLL** up dough starting at long sugared side leaving 1 inch free at opposite side.

5. **CUT*** dough into 18 (1-inch-wide) slices. Make the 1-inch ends into "snail heads," by pinching each side and gently pulling out "antennae." Place snails standing upright on baking sheet.

6. **MELT*** 1 tablespoon butter. Use a spoon or pastry brush to coat each snail with butter.

7. **HEAT*** oven to 350°F. Bake snails 18 to 20 minutes or until golden brown.

8. **MAKE GLAZE:** Stir powdered sugar and 1 or 2 teaspoons milk to make a thick glaze. Drizzle glaze over snails. Serve warm.

Makes 18 snails

*Adult supervision is suggested.

Prep Time: 20 minutes
Bake Time: 20 minutes

Apple Yogurt Muffins

12 REYNOLDS® Baking Cups

Topping

2 tablespoons flour

2 tablespoons sugar

1 tablespoon butter or margarine, softened

$\frac{1}{2}$ teaspoon ground cinnamon

Muffins

2 cups flour

$\frac{1}{2}$ cup sugar

1 tablespoon baking powder

$\frac{1}{2}$ teaspoon salt

$\frac{1}{4}$ teaspoon ground cinnamon

1 carton (8 ounces) low-fat vanilla yogurt

1 egg

$\frac{1}{4}$ cup vegetable oil

2 tablespoons low-fat milk

$\frac{3}{4}$ cup peeled and chopped apples

$\frac{1}{3}$ cup raisins

REYNOLDS® Color Plastic Wrap

PREHEAT oven to 400°F. Place Reynolds Baking Cups in a muffin pan; set aside.

For Topping

COMBINE topping ingredients until crumbly; set aside.

For Muffins

COMBINE flour, sugar, baking powder, salt and cinnamon in large bowl. Beat together yogurt, egg, oil and milk in small bowl. Add to flour mixture; stir just until dry ingredients are moistened. Gently stir in apples and raisins. Spoon batter into baking cups, filling even with top of baking cups. Sprinkle topping over each muffin.

BAKE 23 to 25 minutes or until golden brown. Cool in pan. Wrap muffins individually in plastic wrap. *Makes 12 muffins*

55

Kids' Wrap

4 teaspoons Dijon honey mustard

2 (8-inch) fat-free flour tortillas

2 slices reduced-fat American cheese, torn into halves

4 ounces fat-free oven-roasted turkey breast

½ cup shredded carrots (about 1 medium)

3 romaine lettuce leaves, washed and torn into bite-size
     pieces

1. Spread 2 teaspoons mustard evenly over one tortilla.

2. Top with 2 cheese halves, half of turkey, half of shredded carrots and half of torn lettuce.

3. Roll up tortilla and cut in half. Repeat with remaining ingredients.

Makes 2 servings

Snackin' Cinnamon Popcorn

3 to 4 teaspoons brown sugar substitute

1 ½ teaspoons salt

1 ½ teaspoons cinnamon

8 cups hot air popped popcorn

Butter-flavored nonstick cooking spray

1. Combine brown sugar substitute, salt and cinnamon in small bowl; mix well.

2. Spread hot popped popcorn onto jelly-roll pan; coat with cooking spray and immediately sprinkle cinnamon mixture over popcorn. Serve immediately or store in container at room temperature up to 2 days.

Makes 4 servings (2 cups each)

Peanut Butter-Banana Pops

1 package (16.1 ounces) JELL-O® No Bake Peanut Butter
   Cup Dessert
1⅓ cups cold milk
1 medium banana, chopped

PLACE Topping Pouch in large bowl of boiling water; set aside.

POUR milk into deep, medium bowl. Add Filling Mix and Peanut Butter
Packet. Beat with electric mixer on lowest speed 30 seconds. Beat on
highest speed 3 minutes. (Do not underbeat.) Gently stir in Crust Mix
and banana. Spoon into 12 paper-lined muffin cups.

REMOVE pouch from water. Knead pouch 60 seconds until fluid and no
longer lumpy. Squeeze topping equally over mixture in cups, tilting pan
slightly to coat tops. Insert pop sticks into cups.

FREEZE 2 hours or overnight until firm. Remove paper liners.

Makes 12 pops

Prep Time: 15 minutes
Freeze Time: 2 hours

Super Suggestion!

Wooden pop sticks are sold at
craft and hobby stores.

Inside-Out Turkey Sandwiches

2 tablespoons fat-free cream cheese

2 tablespoons pasteurized process cheese spread

2 teaspoons chopped green onion tops

1 teaspoon prepared mustard

12 thin round slices fat-free turkey breast or smoked turkey breast

4 large pretzel logs or unsalted breadsticks

1. Combine cream cheese, process cheese spread, green onion and mustard in small bowl; mix well.

2. Arrange 3 turkey slices on large sheet of plastic wrap, overlapping slices in center. Spread ¼ of cream cheese mixture evenly onto turkey slices, covering slices completely. Place 1 pretzel at bottom edge of turkey slices; roll up turkey around pretzel. (Be sure to keep all 3 turkey slices together as you roll them around pretzel.)

3. Repeat with remaining ingredients.   *Makes 4 servings*

Peanut Butter 'n' Chocolate Chips Snack Mix

6 cups bite-size crisp corn, rice or wheat squares cereal

3 cups miniature pretzels

2 cups toasted oat cereal rings

1 cup raisins or dried fruit bits

1 cup HERSHEY'S Semi-Sweet Chocolate Chips

1 cup REESE'S® Peanut Butter Chips

Stir together all ingredients in large bowl. Store in airtight container at room temperature.   *Makes 14 cups*

Monster Sandwiches

8 assorted round and oblong sandwich rolls
  Butter
16 to 24 slices assorted cold cuts (salami, turkey, ham, bologna)
 6 to 8 slices assorted cheeses (American, Swiss, Muenster)
 1 firm tomato, sliced
 1 cucumber, sliced thinly
  Assorted lettuce leaves (Romaine, curly, red leaf)
  Cocktail onions
  Green and black olives
  Cherry tomatoes
  Pickled gherkins
  Radishes
  Baby corn
  Hard-cooked eggs

1. Cut rolls open just below center and spread with butter.

2. Layer meats, cheeses, tomato and cucumber slices and greens to make monster faces. Roll "tongues" from ham slices or make "lips" with tomato slices.

3. Use toothpicks to affix remaining ingredients for eyes, ears, fins, horns, hair, etc.

Makes 8 sandwiches

Super Suggestion!

Remember to remove
toothpicks before eating.

Monster Sandwich

Fruit and Oat Squares

1 cup all-purpose flour
1 cup uncooked quick oats
¾ cup packed light brown sugar
½ teaspoon baking soda
¼ teaspoon salt
¼ teaspoon ground cinnamon
⅓ cup margarine or butter, melted
¾ cup apricot, cherry or other fruit flavor preserves

1. Preheat oven to 350°F. Spray 9-inch square baking pan with nonstick cooking spray; set aside.

2. Combine flour, oats, brown sugar, baking soda, salt and cinnamon in medium bowl; mix well. Add margarine; stir with fork until mixture is crumbly. Reserve ¾ cup crumb mixture for topping. Press remaining crumb mixture evenly onto bottom of prepared pan. Bake 5 to 7 minutes or until lightly browned. Spread preserves onto crust; sprinkle with reserved crumb mixture.

3. Bake 20 to 25 minutes or until golden brown. Cool completely in pan on wire rack. Cut into 16 squares.   *Makes 16 servings*

Tip: Store individually wrapped Fruit and Oat Squares at room temperature up to 3 days or freeze up to 1 month.

Stuffed Banana Smiles

1 medium size banana, with peel on

1 tablespoon **SUN-MAID®** Raisins or Golden Raisins

1 tablespoon semi-sweet, milk or white chocolate baking chips

1. **PLACE** banana, with peel on, flat on its side on a microwave-safe plate.

2. **STARTING*** and ending ¼ inch from the ends of banana, cut a slit lengthwise through the banana up to the skin on the other side.

3. **GENTLY** open the banana. Use your fingers to stuff the banana with raisins, then add chocolate chips.

4. **MICROWAVE*** banana uncovered on HIGH for 40 to 60 seconds or until chocolate begins to melt and banana is still firm. Banana skin may darken slightly. Eat immediately, scooping with a spoon right out of the banana peel.   *Makes 1 serving*

*Adult supervision is suggested.

Tip: At a party, invite guests to prepare their own banana smile!

Tip: On your grill,* place each banana flat on its side, on a piece of aluminum foil and follow steps 2 and 3 above. Wrap bananas loosely and pinch foil closed. Place on covered barbecue grill or over hot coals for about 5 minutes or just until chocolate begins to melt and banana is still firm.

Tip: Place wrapped bananas on a baking sheet and bake in the oven* at 350°F for 5 minutes.

Prep Time: 2 minutes
Bake Time: 1 minute

Peanut Butter Chip-Granola Bars

¼ cup (½ stick) butter or margarine, softened
¼ cup shortening
1 cup packed light brown sugar
1 egg
1 teaspoon vanilla extract
1⅓ cups all-purpose flour
½ teaspoon baking soda
½ teaspoon ground cinnamon
½ teaspoon salt
¼ cup milk
1⅔ cups granola or natural cereal, crumbled
1 cup MOUNDS® Sweetened Coconut Flakes
1 cup raisins
1⅔ cups (10-ounce package) REESE'S® Peanut Butter Chips

1. Heat oven to 350°F. Line 15½×10½×1-inch jelly-roll pan with foil.

2. Beat butter, shortening, brown sugar, egg and vanilla in large bowl until well blended. Stir together flour, baking soda, cinnamon and salt; add alternately with milk to butter mixture, beating until well blended. Stir in granola, coconut, raisins and peanut butter chips. Spread batter into prepared pan.

3. Bake 20 to 25 minutes or until top is golden brown. Cool completely in pan on wire rack. Invert pan; peel off foil. Cut into bars.

Makes about 48 bars

Mini Chip Granola Bars: Substitute HERSHEY®S MINI CHIPS Semi-Sweet Chocolate Chips for peanut butter chips.

Snacking Surprise Muffins

1 ½ cups all-purpose flour

1 cup fresh or frozen blueberries

½ cup sugar

2 ½ teaspoons baking powder

1 teaspoon ground cinnamon

¼ teaspoon salt

⅔ cup buttermilk

1 egg, beaten

¼ cup margarine or butter, melted

3 tablespoons peach preserves

Topping

1 tablespoon sugar

¼ teaspoon ground cinnamon

1. Preheat oven to 400°F. Line 12 medium muffin cups with paper liners; set aside.

2. Combine flour, blueberries, ½ cup sugar, baking powder, 1 teaspoon cinnamon and salt in medium bowl. Combine buttermilk, egg and margarine in small bowl. Add to flour mixture; mix just until moistened.

3. Spoon about 1 tablespoon batter into each muffin cup. Drop a scant teaspoonful of preserves into center of batter in each cup; top with remaining batter.

4. Combine 1 tablespoon sugar and ¼ teaspoon cinnamon in small bowl; sprinkle evenly over tops of batter.

5. Bake 18 to 20 minutes or until lightly browned. Remove muffins to wire rack to cool completely.   *Makes 12 servings*

Bologna "Happy Faces"

4 slices whole wheat or rye bread

1 cup prepared oil and vinegar based coleslaw

8 ounces **HEBREW NATIONAL®** Sliced Lean Beef Bologna or Lean Beef Salami

4 large pimiento-stuffed green olives

HEBREW NATIONAL® Deli Mustard

For each sandwich, spread 1 bread slice with 3 tablespoons coleslaw; top with 5 slices bologna. Cut olives in half crosswise; place over bologna for "eyes." Draw smiley "mouth" with mustard. Drop 1 tablespoon coleslaw at top of face for "hair." *Makes 4 open-faced sandwiches*

Tuna Supper Sandwiches

2 cups shredded Cheddar cheese

1/3 cup chopped green onions, including tops

1/3 cup chopped red bell pepper

1 can (2 1/4 ounces) sliced ripe olives, drained

2 tablespoons minced fresh parsley

1 teaspoon curry powder

Seasoned salt to taste

1 (7-ounce) pouch of **STARKIST®** Premium Albacore or Chunk Light Tuna

1/2 cup light mayonnaise

6 soft French rolls (7 inches *each*), halved lengthwise

In medium bowl, place cheese, onions, red pepper, olives, parsley, curry powder and seasoned salt; mix lightly. Add tuna and mayonnaise; toss lightly with fork. Cover baking sheet with foil; place rolls on foil. Spread about 1/3 cup mixture on each half. Bake in 450°F oven 10 to 12 minutes or until tops are bubbling and beginning to brown. Cool slightly before serving. *Makes 12 servings*

Sub on the Run

2 hard rolls (2 ounces each), split into halves
4 tomato slices
14 turkey pepperoni slices
2 ounces fat-free oven-roasted turkey breast
¼ cup (1 ounce) shredded part-skim mozzarella
1 cup packaged coleslaw mix or shredded lettuce
¼ medium green bell pepper, thinly sliced
2 tablespoons prepared fat-free Italian salad dressing

Top each of two bottom halves of rolls with 2 tomato slices, 7 pepperoni slices, half of turkey, 2 tablespoons cheese, ½ of coleslaw mix and half of bell pepper slices. Top with dressing and roll tops. *Makes 2 servings*

Old-Fashioned Pop Corn Balls

2 quarts popped JOLLY TIME® Pop Corn
1 cup sugar
⅓ cup light or dark corn syrup
⅓ cup water
¼ cup butter or margarine
½ teaspoon salt
1 teaspoon vanilla

Keep popped pop corn warm in 200°F oven. In 2-quart saucepan, stir together sugar, corn syrup, water, butter and salt. Cook over medium heat, stirring constantly, until mixture comes to a boil. Continue cooking without stirring until temperature reaches 270°F on candy thermometer or until small amount of syrup dropped into very cold water separates into threads which are hard but not brittle. Remove from heat. Add vanilla; stir just enough to mix through hot syrup. Slowly pour over popped pop corn, stirring to coat well. Cool just enough to handle. With JOLLY TIME® Pop Corn Ball Maker or buttered hands, shape into balls.

Makes 12 medium-sized pop corn balls

Taco Popcorn Olé

9 cups air-popped popcorn
Butter-flavored cooking spray
1 teaspoon chili powder
½ teaspoon salt
½ teaspoon garlic powder
⅛ teaspoon ground red pepper (optional)

1. Preheat oven to 350°F. Line 15×10-inch jelly-roll pan with foil.

2. Place popcorn in single layer in prepared pan. Coat lightly with cooking spray.

3. Combine chili powder, salt, garlic powder and red pepper, if desired, in small bowl; sprinkle over popcorn. Mix lightly to coat evenly.

4. Bake 5 minutes or until hot, stirring gently after 3 minutes. Spread mixture in single layer on large sheet of foil to cool.

Makes 6 (1½-cup) servings

Tip: Store popcorn mixture in tightly covered container at room temperature up to 4 days.

Sun-Maid® Apricot Pops

1 (6-ounce) package SUN-MAID® Mediterranean Apricots

28 pretzel sticks about 4 inches long and ³⁄₈ inch thick

1 cup (6 ounces) semi-sweet or white chocolate baking chips, or ½ cup of each

Decorating Supplies

1 package SUN-MAID® Fruit Bits or Tropical Medley

Cookie sprinkles

1. **PLACE** a piece of wax paper or plastic wrap on a cookie sheet and set aside.

2. **PUSH** a pretzel stick into the small opening at the edge of each apricot.

3. **PUT*** chocolate in a microwave-safe bowl, or separate bowls for each type of chocolate. Heat on medium power (50%) for about 2 minutes. Stir until chips are melted.

4. **HOLD** end of pretzels and dip apricots, one at a time, into chocolate.

5. **DECORATE** each "Apricot Pop" right after dipping:

- Roll in a dish of SUN-MAID® Fruit Bits or Tropical Medley.

- Sprinkle with cookie sprinkles.

- Dip a toothpick in chocolate to drizzle stripes or designs.

- Make up your own decoration, or leave it plain chocolate!

6. Place finished "Apricot Pops" on cookie sheet. Refrigerate 10 minutes until chocolate is set.   *Makes about 28 pops*

*Adult supervision is suggested.

Prep Time: 20 minutes

Savory Pita Chips

2 whole wheat or white pita bread rounds
   Olive oil-flavored nonstick cooking spray
3 tablespoons grated Parmesan cheese
I teaspoon dried basil leaves
¼ teaspoon garlic powder

1. Preheat oven to 350°F. Line baking sheet with foil; set aside.

2. Using small scissors, carefully split each pita bread round around edges; separate to form 2 rounds. Cut each round into 6 wedges.

3. Place wedges, rough side down, on prepared baking sheet; coat lightly with cooking spray. Turn wedges over; spray again.

4. Combine Parmesan cheese, basil and garlic powder in small bowl; sprinkle evenly over pita wedges.

5. Bake 12 to 14 minutes or until golden brown. Cool completely.

Makes 4 servings

Cinnamon Crisps: Substitute butter-flavored cooking spray for olive oil-flavored cooking spray and I tablespoon sugar mixed with ¼ teaspoon ground cinnamon for Parmesan cheese, basil and garlic powder.

Sassy Southwestern Veggie Wraps

½ cup diced zucchini

½ cup diced red or yellow bell pepper

½ cup frozen corn, thawed

1 jalapeño pepper,* seeded and chopped (optional)

¾ cup shredded reduced-fat Mexican cheese blend

3 tablespoons prepared salsa or picante sauce

2 (8-inch) fat-free flour tortillas

*Jalapeño peppers can sting and irritate the skin; wear rubber gloves when handling peppers and do not touch eyes. Wash hands after handling peppers.

1. Combine zucchini, bell pepper, corn and jalapeño pepper, if desired, in small bowl. Stir in cheese and salsa; mix well.

2. Soften tortillas according to package directions. Spoon vegetable mixture down center of tortillas, distributing evenly; roll up burrito-style. Serve wraps cold or warm.**

Makes 2 servings

**To warm each wrap, cover loosely with plastic wrap and microwave at HIGH 40 to 45 seconds or until cheese is melted.

● ● ● ● ● ● ● ● ● ● ● ●

What do you call a carrot who talks back to a farmer?

● ● ● ● ● ● ● ● ● ● ● ●

Answer: A fresh vegetable!

Sassy Southwestern Veggie Wrap

Rock 'n' Rollers

4 (6- to 7-inch) flour tortillas
4 ounces Neufchâtel cheese, softened
⅓ cup peach preserves
1 cup (4 ounces) shredded fat-free Cheddar cheese
½ cup packed washed fresh spinach leaves
3 ounces thinly sliced regular or smoked turkey breast

1. Spread each tortilla evenly with 1 ounce Neufchâtel cheese; cover with thin layer of preserves. Sprinkle with Cheddar cheese.

2. Arrange spinach leaves and turkey over Cheddar cheese. Roll up tortillas; trim ends. Cover and refrigerate until ready to serve.

3. Cut "rollers" crosswise in half or diagonally into 1-inch pieces.

Makes 4 servings

Sassy Salsa Rollers: Substitute salsa for peach preserves and shredded iceberg lettuce for spinach leaves.

Ham 'n' Apple Rollers: Omit peach preserves and spinach leaves. Substitute lean ham slices for turkey. Spread tortillas with Neufchâtel cheese as directed; sprinkle with Cheddar cheese. Top each tortilla with about 2 tablespoons finely chopped apple and 2 ham slices; roll up. Continue as directed.

Wedgies: Prepare Rock 'n' Rollers or any variation as directed, but do not roll up. Top with second tortilla; cut into wedges. Continue as directed.

Light Bites

Double-Sauced Chicken Pizza Bagels

1 whole bagel (about 3½ ounces), split in half
4 tablespoons prepared pizza sauce
½ cup diced cooked chicken breast
¼ cup (1 ounce) shredded part-skim mozzarella cheese
2 teaspoons grated Parmesan cheese

1. Place bagel halves on microwavable plate.

2. Spoon 1 tablespoon pizza sauce onto each bagel half. Spread evenly using back of spoon.

3. Top each bagel half with ¼ cup chicken. Spoon 1 tablespoon pizza sauce over chicken on each bagel half.

4. Sprinkle 2 tablespoons mozzarella cheese over top of each bagel half.

5. Cover bagel halves loosely with waxed paper and microwave at HIGH 1 to 1½ minutes or until cheese melts.

6. Carefully remove waxed paper. Sprinkle each bagel half with 1 teaspoon Parmesan cheese. Let stand 1 minute before eating to cool slightly. (Bagels will be very hot.)   *Makes 2 servings (1 bagel half each)*

Tip: For crunchier "pizzas," toast bagels before adding toppings.

Surfin' Salmon

⅓ cup cornflake crumbs

⅓ cup cholesterol-free egg substitute

2 tablespoons fat-free (skim) milk

¾ teaspoon dried dill weed

⅛ teaspoon black pepper

Dash hot pepper sauce

1 (14½-ounce) can salmon, drained and skin and bones removed

Nonstick cooking spray

1 teaspoon olive oil

6 tablespoons purchased tartar sauce

5 small pieces pimiento

1. Stir together cornflake crumbs, egg substitute, milk, dill weed, black pepper and hot pepper sauce in large mixing bowl. Add salmon; mix well.

2. Spray large nonstick skillet with cooking spray. Shape salmon mixture into 5 large egg-shaped balls. Flatten each into ¾-inch-thick oval. Pinch one end of each oval into tail shape for fish.

3. Cook in skillet over medium-high heat 2 to 3 minutes or until lightly browned; turn. Add oil to skillet. Continue cooking 2 to 3 minutes or until firm and lightly browned.

4. Place small drop tartar sauce and pimiento on each for "eye." Serve with remaining tartar sauce, if desired.   *Makes 5 servings*

Tip: Serve romaine lettuce on the side of the Surfin' Salmon patty to add the look of sea plants. What a fun way to get your little one to eat fresh vegetables!

Creamy Strawberry-Orange Pops

1 container (8 ounces) strawberry-flavored yogurt with aspartame sweetener

¾ cup orange juice

2 teaspoons vanilla

2 cups frozen whole strawberries

1 packet sugar substitute *or* equivalent of 2 teaspoons sugar

6 (7-ounce) paper cups

6 wooden sticks

1. Combine yogurt, orange juice and vanilla in food processor or blender. Cover and blend until smooth.

2. Add frozen strawberries and sugar substitute. Blend until smooth. Pour into 6 paper cups, filling each about ¾ full. Place in freezer for 1 hour. Insert wooden stick into center of each. Freeze completely. Peel cup off each to serve. *Makes 6 servings*

Stuffed Bundles

1 package (10 ounces) refrigerated pizza dough

2 ounces lean ham or turkey ham, chopped

½ cup (2 ounces) shredded reduced-fat sharp Cheddar cheese

1. Preheat oven to 425°F. Coat nonstick 12-cup muffin pan with nonstick cooking spray.

2. Unroll dough on flat surface; cut into 12 pieces, about 4×3-inch rectangles.

3. Divide ham and cheese between dough rectangles. Bring corners of dough together, pinching to seal. Place, smooth side up, in prepared muffin cups.

4. Bake 10 to 12 minutes or until golden. *Makes 12 servings*

86

Dreamy Orange Cheesecake Dip

1 package (8 ounces) reduced-fat cream cheese, softened
½ cup orange marmalade
½ teaspoon vanilla
Grated orange peel (optional)
Mint leaves (optional)
2 cups whole strawberries
2 cups cantaloupe chunks
2 cups apple slices

1. Combine cheese, marmalade and vanilla in small bowl; mix well. Garnish with orange zest and mint leaves, if desired.

2. Serve with fruit dippers. *Makes 12 servings*

Note: Dip may be prepared ahead of time. Store, covered, in refrigerator for up to 2 days.

Frozen Fudge Pops

½ cup nonfat sweetened condensed milk
¼ cup unsweetened cocoa powder
1¼ cups nonfat evaporated milk
1 teaspoon vanilla

1. Beat together sweetened condensed milk and cocoa in medium bowl. Add evaporated milk and vanilla; beat until smooth.

2. Pour mixture into 8 small paper cups or 8 popsicle molds. Freeze about 2 hours or until beginning to set. Insert wooden popsicle sticks; freeze solid. *Makes 8 servings*

Peanut Pitas

1 package (8 ounces) small pita breads, cut crosswise in half
16 teaspoons reduced-fat peanut butter
16 teaspoons strawberry spreadable fruit
1 large banana, peeled and thinly sliced (about 48 slices)

1. Spread inside of each pita half with 1 teaspoon each peanut butter and spreadable fruit.

2. Fill pita halves evenly with banana slices. Serve immediately.

Makes 8 servings

Honey Bees: Substitute honey for spreadable fruit.

Jolly Jellies: Substitute any flavor jelly for spreadable fruit and thin apple slices for banana slices.

P. B. Crunchers: Substitute reduced-fat mayonnaise for spreadable fruit and celery slices for banana slices.

Banana Tot Pops

3 firm, medium DOLE® Bananas
6 large wooden sticks
½ cup raspberry or other flavored yogurt
1 jar (1¾ ounces) chocolate or rainbow sprinkles

• Cut each banana crosswise in half. Insert wooden stick into each half.

• Pour yogurt into small bowl. Hold banana pop over bowl; spoon yogurt to cover all sides of banana. Allow excess yogurt to drip into bowl. Sprinkle candies over yogurt.

• Place pops on wax paper-lined tray. Freeze 2 hours.

Makes 6 servings

Prep Time: 20 minutes
Freeze Time: 2 hours

90

Peanut Pitas

Brontosaurus Bites

4 cups air-popped popcorn

2 cups mini-dinosaur grahams

2 cups corn cereal squares

1½ cups dried pineapple wedges

1 package (6 ounces) dried fruit bits

Butter-flavored nonstick cooking spray

1 tablespoon plus 1½ teaspoons sugar

1½ teaspoons ground cinnamon

½ teaspoon ground nutmeg

1 cup yogurt-covered raisins

1. Preheat oven to 350°F. Combine popcorn, grahams, cereal, pineapple and fruit bits in large bowl; mix lightly. Transfer to 15×10-inch jelly-roll pan. Spray mixture generously with cooking spray.

2. Combine sugar, cinnamon and nutmeg in small bowl. Sprinkle ½ of sugar mixture over popcorn mixture; toss lightly to coat. Spray mixture again with additional cooking spray. Add remaining sugar mixture; mix lightly.

3. Bake snack mix 10 minutes, stirring after 5 minutes. Cool completely in pan on wire rack. Add raisins; mix lightly.

Makes 12 (¾-cup) servings

Gorilla Grub: Substitute plain raisins for the yogurt-covered raisins and ¼ cup grated Parmesan cheese for the sugar, cinnamon and nutmeg.

Super Suggestion!

For individual party take-home treats, wrap snack mix in festive colored paper napkins.

Warm Peanut-Caramel Dip

¼ **cup reduced-fat peanut butter**

2 **tablespoons fat-free caramel topping**

2 **tablespoons fat-free (skim) milk**

1 **large apple, thinly sliced**

4 **large pretzel rods, broken in half**

1. Combine peanut butter, caramel topping and milk in small saucepan. Heat over low heat, stirring constantly, until mixture is melted and warm.

2. Serve dip with apple slices and pretzel rods.   *Makes 4 servings*

Microwave Directions: Combine all ingredients except apple slices and pretzel rods in small microwavable dish. Microwave at MEDIUM (50%) 1 minute; stir well. Microwave an additional minute or until mixture is melted and warm. Serve dip with apple slices and pretzel rods.

Cheesy Chips

10 **wonton wrappers**

2 **tablespoons powdered American cheese or grated Parmesan cheese**

2 **teaspoons olive oil**

⅛ **teaspoon garlic powder**

1. Preheat oven to 375°F. Spray baking sheet with nonstick cooking spray.

2. Diagonally cut each wonton wrapper in half, forming two triangles. Place in single layer on prepared baking sheet.

3. Combine cheese, oil and garlic powder in small bowl. Sprinkle over wonton triangles.

4. Bake 6 to 8 minutes or until golden brown and crisp. Remove from oven. Cool completely.   *Makes 4 servings*

Señor Nacho Dip

4 ounces fat-free cream cheese

½ cup (2 ounces) reduced-fat Cheddar cheese

¼ cup mild or medium chunky salsa

2 teaspoons low-fat (2%) milk

4 ounces baked tortilla chips or assorted fresh vegetable dippers

1. Combine cream cheese and Cheddar cheese in small saucepan; stir over low heat until melted. Stir in salsa and milk; heat thoroughly, stirring occasionally.

2. Transfer dip to small serving bowl. Serve with tortilla chips. Garnish with hot peppers and cilantro, if desired. *Makes 4 servings*

Olé Dip: Substitute reduced-fat Monterey Jack cheese or taco cheese for Cheddar cheese.

Spicy Mustard Dip: Omit tortilla chips. Substitute 2 teaspoons spicy brown or honey mustard for salsa. Serve with fresh vegetable dippers or pretzels.

Banana S'mores

1 firm DOLE® Banana, sliced

12 graham cracker squares

6 large marshmallows

1 bar (1.55 ounces) milk chocolate candy

Microwave Directions

• Arrange 4 banana slices on each of 6 graham cracker squares. Top with marshmallow. Microwave on HIGH 12 to 15 seconds or until puffed.

• Place 2 squares chocolate on remaining 6 graham crackers. Microwave on HIGH 1 minute or until just soft. Put halves together to make sandwich. *Makes 6 servings*

Prep Time: 5 minutes
Cook Time: 1 minute

94

Cinnamon-Raisin Roll-Ups

> 4 ounces reduced-fat cream cheese, softened
> 1/2 cup shredded carrot
> 1/4 cup golden raisins
> 1 tablespoon honey
> 1/4 teaspoon ground cinnamon
> 4 (7- to 8-inch) whole wheat or regular flour tortillas
> 8 thin apple wedges (optional)

1. Combine cream cheese, carrot, raisins, honey and cinnamon in small bowl; mix well.

2. Spread tortillas evenly with cream cheese mixture, leaving 1/2-inch border around edge of each tortilla. Place 2 apple wedges down center of each tortilla; roll up. Wrap in plastic wrap. Refrigerate until ready to serve or pack in lunch box.   *Makes 4 servings*

Tip: For extra convenience, prepare roll-ups the night before. In the morning, pack roll-up in lunch box along with a frozen juice box. The juice box will be thawed by lunchtime and will keep the snack cold in the meantime!

Peanut Butter-Pineapple Celery Sticks

> 1/2 cup low-fat (1%) cottage cheese
> 1/2 cup reduced-fat peanut butter
> 1/2 cup crushed pineapple in juice, drained
> 12 (3-inch-long) celery sticks

Combine cottage cheese and peanut butter in food processor. Blend until smooth. Stir in pineapple. Stuff celery sticks with mixture.

Makes 6 servings

Serving Suggestion: Substitute 2 medium apples, sliced, for celery.

Finger Lickin' Chicken Salad

½ cup purchased carved roasted skinless chicken breast
½ rib celery, cut into 1-inch pieces
¼ cup drained mandarin orange segments
¼ cup red seedless grapes
2 tablespoons fat-free sugar-free lemon yogurt
1 tablespoon reduced-fat mayonnaise
¼ teaspoon reduced-sodium soy sauce
⅛ teaspoon pumpkin pie spice or cinnamon

1. Toss together chicken, celery, oranges and grapes. Place in covered plastic container.

2. For dipping sauce, stir together yogurt, mayonnaise, soy sauce and pumpkin pie spice.

3. Pack chicken mixture and dipping sauce in insulated bag with ice pack. To serve, dip chicken mixture into dipping sauce.

Makes 1 serving

Tip: Alternately thread the chicken, celery, oranges and grapes on wooden skewers for a creative variation to this recipe.

Sloppy Joe's Bun Buggy

      4 hot dog buns (not split)
     16 thin slices cucumber or zucchini
     24 thin strips julienned carrots, 1 inch long
      4 ripe olives or pimiento-stuffed olives
        Nonstick cooking spray
      1 (10-ounce) package extra-lean ground turkey
  1¼ cups bottled reduced-fat spaghetti sauce
   ½ cup chopped broccoli stems
      2 teaspoons prepared mustard
   ½ teaspoon Worcestershire sauce
        Dash salt
        Dash black pepper
      4 small pretzel twists

1. Hollow out hot dog buns. Use wooden pick to make four holes in sides of each bun to attach "wheels." Use wooden pick to make one hole in center of each cucumber slice; push carrot strip through hole. Press into holes in buns, making "wheels" on buns.

2. Cut each olive in half horizontally. Use wooden pick to make two holes in one end of each bun to attach "headlights." Use carrot strips to attach olives to buns, making "headlights."

3. Spray large nonstick skillet with cooking spray. Cook turkey in skillet over medium heat until no longer pink. Stir in spaghetti sauce, broccoli stems, mustard, Worcestershire, salt and pepper; heat through.

4. Spoon sauce mixture into hollowed-out buns. Press pretzel twist into ground turkey mixture, making "windshield" on each buggy.

Makes 4 servings

One Potato, Two Potato

Nonstick cooking spray

2 medium baking potatoes, cut lengthwise into 4 wedges
Salt

½ cup unseasoned dry bread crumbs

2 tablespoons grated Parmesan cheese (optional)

1½ teaspoons dried oregano leaves, dill weed, Italian herbs or paprika

Spicy brown or honey mustard, ketchup or reduced-fat sour cream

1. Preheat oven to 425°F. Spray baking sheet with nonstick cooking spray; set aside.

2. Spray cut sides of potatoes generously with cooking spray; sprinkle lightly with salt.

3. Combine bread crumbs, Parmesan cheese and desired herb in shallow dish. Add potatoes; toss lightly until potatoes are generously coated with crumb mixture. Place on prepared baking sheet.

4. Bake potatoes until browned and tender, about 20 minutes. Serve warm as dippers with mustard. *Makes 4 servings*

Potato Sweets: Omit Parmesan cheese, herbs and mustard. Substitute sweet potatoes for baking potatoes. Cut and spray potatoes as directed; coat generously with desired amount of cinnamon-sugar. Bake as directed. Serve warm as dippers with peach or pineapple preserves or honey mustard.

● ● ● ● ● ● ● ● ● ● ● ●

What kind of toes do people like to eat?

● ● ● ● ● ● ● ● ● ● ● ●

Answer: Tomatoes and potatoes.

Little Piggy Pies

2 cups frozen mixed soup vegetables (carrots, potatoes, peas, celery, green beans, corn, onions and lima beans)

1 (10¾-ounce) can reduced-fat condensed cream of chicken soup, undiluted

8 ounces chopped cooked chicken

⅓ cup plain low-fat yogurt

⅓ cup water

½ teaspoon dried thyme leaves

¼ teaspoon poultry seasoning or ground sage

⅛ teaspoon garlic powder

1 (7½-ounce) tube (10) refrigerated buttermilk biscuits

1. Preheat oven to 400°F.

2. Remove 10 green peas from frozen mixed vegetables; set aside. Stir together remaining frozen vegetables, soup, chicken, yogurt, water, thyme, poultry seasoning and garlic powder in medium saucepan. Bring to a boil, stirring frequently. Cover; keep warm.

3. Press five biscuits into 3-inch circles. Cut each remaining biscuit into eight wedges. Place two wedges on top of each circle; fold points down to form ears. Roll one wedge into small ball; place in center of each circle to form pig's snout. Use tip of spoon handle to make indents in snout for nostrils. Place 2 reserved green peas on each circle for eyes.

4. Spoon hot chicken mixture into 5 (10-ounce) custard cups. Place one biscuit "pig" on top of each. Place remaining biscuit wedges around each "pig" on top of chicken mixture, twisting one wedge "tail" for each. Bake 9 to 11 minutes or until biscuits are golden.   *Makes 5 servings*

Prep Time: 10 minutes
Bake Time: 11 minutes

Confetti Tuna in Celery Sticks

1 (3-ounce) pouch of STARKIST® Premium Albacore or
    Chunk Light Tuna

½ cup shredded red or green cabbage

½ cup shredded carrot

¼ cup shredded yellow squash or zucchini

3 tablespoons reduced-calorie cream cheese, softened

1 tablespoon plain low-fat yogurt

½ teaspoon dried basil, crushed

    Salt and pepper to taste

10 to 12 (4-inch) celery sticks, with leaves if desired

1. In a small bowl toss together tuna, cabbage, carrot and squash.

2. Stir in cream cheese, yogurt and basil. Add salt and pepper to taste.

3. With small spatula spread mixture evenly into celery sticks.

Makes 10 to 12 servings

Tuna Schooners

2 (3-ounce) cans water-packed light tuna, drained

½ cup finely chopped apple

¼ cup shredded carrot

⅓ cup reduced-fat ranch salad dressing

2 English muffins, split and lightly toasted

8 triangular-shaped baked whole wheat crackers or
    triangular-shaped tortilla chips

1. Combine tuna, apple and carrot in medium bowl. Add salad dressing; stir to combine.

2. Spread ¼ of tuna mixture over top of each muffin half. Stand 2 crackers and press firmly into tuna mixture on each muffin half to form 'sails.'

Makes 4 servings

Peach Freezies

1½ cups (12 ounces) canned or thawed frozen peach slices, drained

¾ cup peach nectar

1 tablespoon sugar

¼ to ½ teaspoon coconut extract (optional)

1. Place peaches, nectar, sugar and extract, if desired, in food processor or blender container; process until smooth.

2. Spoon 2 tablespoons fruit mixture into each section of ice cube trays.*

3. Freeze until almost firm. Insert toothpick into each cube; freeze until firm.   *Makes 12 servings*

Or, pour ⅓ cup fruit mixture into each of 8 plastic pop molds or small paper or plastic cups. Freeze until almost firm. Insert wooden stick into each mold; freeze until firm. Makes 8 servings.

Apricot Freezies: Substitute canned apricot halves for peach slices and apricot nectar for peach nectar.

Pear Freezies: Substitute canned pear slices for peach slices, pear nectar for peach nectar and almond extract for coconut extract.

Pineapple Freezies: Substitute crushed pineapple for peach slices and unsweetened pineapple juice for peach nectar.

Mango Freezies: Substitute chopped fresh mango for canned peach slices and mango nectar for peach nectar. Omit coconut extract.

Fantasy Cinnamon Applewiches

   4 raisin bread slices
   ⅓ cup reduced-fat cream cheese
   ¼ cup finely chopped unpeeled apple
   1 teaspoon sugar
   ⅛ teaspoon ground cinnamon

1. Toast bread. Cut into desired shapes using large cookie cutters.

2. Combine cream cheese and apple in small bowl; spread onto toast.

3. Combine sugar and cinnamon in another small bowl; sprinkle evenly over cream cheese mixture. *Makes 4 servings*

Tip: Get out the cookie cutters any time of the year for this fun treat. Or, create your own fun shapes—be sure to have an adult cut out your requested shape with a serrated knife for best results.

Sweet Nothings Trail Mix

   5 cups rice and corn cereal squares
   1½ cups raisins
   1½ cups small thin pretzel sticks, broken into pieces
   1 cup candy-coated chocolate candy
   1 cup peanuts

1. Have children decorate small resealable food storage bags with Valentine's Day or other holiday stickers, if desired.

2. Combine cereal, raisins, pretzels, candy and peanuts in large resealable plastic food storage bag; shake well. Distribute evenly among decorated bags or serve in large bowl. *Makes 10 cups*

Prep Time: 10 minutes

Hidden Pumpkin Pie

1½ cups canned solid-pack pumpkin
1 cup evaporated skimmed milk
½ cup cholesterol-free egg substitute
¼ cup no-calorie sweetener
1 teaspoon pumpkin pie spice
1¼ teaspoons vanilla, divided
3 egg whites
¼ teaspoon cream of tartar
⅓ cup honey

1. Preheat oven to 350°F.

2. Stir together pumpkin, evaporated milk, egg substitute, sweetener, pumpkin pie spice and 1 teaspoon vanilla. Pour into 6 (6-ounce) custard cups or 6 (¾-cup) soufflé dishes. Place in shallow baking dish or pan. Pour boiling water around custard cups or soufflé dishes to depth of 1 inch. Bake 25 minutes.

3. Meanwhile, beat egg whites, cream of tartar and remaining ¼ teaspoon vanilla on high speed of electric mixer until soft peaks form. Gradually add honey; continue beating on high speed until stiff peaks form.

4. Spread egg white mixture on top of hot pumpkin mixture. Return to oven. Bake 15 to 16 minutes or until tops are golden brown. Let stand 10 minutes. Serve warm. *Makes 6 servings*

When are cooks very cruel?

Answer: When they beat the eggs and whip the cream.

Banana Freezer Pops

2 ripe medium bananas

1 can (6 ounces) frozen orange juice concentrate, thawed (¾ cup)

¼ cup water

1 tablespoon honey

1 teaspoon vanilla

8 (3-ounce) paper or plastic cups

8 wooden sticks

1. Peel bananas; break into chunks. Place in food processor or blender container.

2. Add orange juice concentrate, water, honey and vanilla; process until smooth.

3. Pour banana mixture evenly into cups. Cover top of each cup with small piece of aluminum foil. Insert wooden stick through center of foil into banana mixture.

4. Place cups on tray; freeze until firm, about 3 hours. To serve, remove foil; tear off paper cups (or slide out of plastic cups).

Makes 8 servings

Peppy Purple Pops: Omit honey and vanilla. Substitute grape juice concentrate for orange juice concentrate.

Frozen Banana Shakes: Increase water to 1½ cups. Prepare fruit mixture as directed. Add 4 ice cubes; process on high speed until mixture is thick and creamy. Makes 3 servings.

Peanut Butter & Jelly Shakes

1½ cups vanilla ice cream
¼ cup milk
2 tablespoons creamy peanut butter
6 peanut butter sandwich cookies, coarsely chopped
¼ cup strawberry preserves

1. Place ice cream, milk and peanut butter in blender. Blend on medium speed 1 to 2 minutes or until smooth and well blended. Add cookie pieces and blend 10 seconds on low speed. Pour into 2 serving glasses.

2. Place preserves and 1 to 2 teaspoons water in small bowl; stir until smooth. Stir 2 tablespoons preserve mixture into each glass. Serve immediately.   *Makes 2 servings*

Serve It With Style!: For a change of pace, prepare these shakes using different flavors of preserves.

Cook's Notes: Eat this thick and creamy shake with a spoon for a mouthful of cookies in every bite.

Prep Time: 10 minutes

"Moo-vin" Chocolate Milk Shakes

I pint low-fat sugar-free chocolate ice cream
½ cup fat-free (skim) milk
I tablespoon chocolate syrup
¼ teaspoon vanilla
⅛ teaspoon decorator sprinkles (optional)

Combine all ingredients except decorator sprinkles in blender container. Cover and blend until smooth. Pour into 2 small glasses. Add decorator sprinkles, if desired. Serve immediately.   *Makes 2 servings*

Cherry-Berry Smoothie

I cup frozen whole unsweetened pitted dark sweet cherries
I cup frozen whole unsweetened strawberries
I cup cranberry-cherry juice

In blender, purée frozen pitted dark sweet cherries, frozen strawberries and juice, stirring as needed, until smooth.
Makes I (16-ounce) serving

Note: Frozen pitted dark sweet cherries may be replaced with ¾ cup well-drained canned pitted dark sweet cherries and four ice cubes.

Favorite recipe from **National Cherry Growers**

Clockwise from top left: "Moo-vin" Chocolate Milk Shake, "Moo-vin" Vanilla Milk Shake (page 122) and "Moo-vin" Strawberry Milk Shake (page 127)

Sparkling Apple Punch

2 bottles (750 mL each) sparkling apple cider, chilled
1½ quarts papaya or apricot nectar, chilled
    Ice
1 or 2 papayas, peeled and chopped
    Orange slices, quartered

Combine apple cider, papaya nectar and ice in punch bowl. Add papaya and orange slices. *Makes about 4 quarts*

Chocolate Root Beer Float

1 tablespoon sugar
2 teaspoons HERSHEY'S Cocoa
1 tablespoon hot water
1 scoop vanilla ice cream
    Cold root beer

1. Stir together sugar and cocoa in 12-ounce glass; stir in water.

2. Add ice cream and enough root beer to half fill glass; stir gently. Fill glass with root beer. Stir; serve immediately.

Makes one (12-ounce) serving

● ● ● ● ● ● ● ● ● ● ● ●

Why did the jelly roll?

● ● ● ● ● ● ● ● ● ●

Answer: Because it saw the apple turnover.

Bottom to top: Sparkling Apple Punch, Citrus Punch (page 121)

Choco-Berry Cooler

¾ cup cold milk

¼ cup sliced fresh strawberries

2 tablespoons HERSHEY'S Syrup

2 tablespoons plus 2 small scoops vanilla ice cream, divided

Cold ginger ale or club soda

Fresh strawberry

Mint leaves (optional)

1. Place milk, strawberries, chocolate syrup and 2 tablespoons ice cream in blender container. Cover and blend until smooth.

2. Alternate remaining 2 scoops of ice cream and chocolate mixture in tall ice cream soda glass; fill glass with ginger ale. Garnish with a fresh strawberry and mint leaves, if desired. Serve immediately.

Makes one (14-ounce) serving

Variations: Before blending, substitute one of the following fruits for fresh strawberries:

• 3 tablespoons frozen strawberries with syrup, thawed

• ½ peeled fresh peach *or* ⅓ cup canned peach slices

• 2 slices canned *or* ¼ cup canned crushed pineapple

• ¼ cup sweetened fresh raspberries *or* 3 tablespoons frozen raspberries with syrup, thawed

Citrus Punch

4 oranges, sectioned

I to 2 limes, cut into ⅛-inch slices

I lemon, cut into ⅛-inch slices

I pint strawberries, stemmed and halved

I cup raspberries

2 cups orange juice

2 cups grapefruit juice

¾ cup lime juice

½ cup light corn syrup

I bottle (750 mL) ginger ale, white grape juice, Asti Spumante or sparkling wine

Fresh mint sprigs for garnish

Spread oranges, limes, lemon, strawberries and raspberries on baking sheet. Freeze 4 hours or until firm.

Combine juices and corn syrup in 2-quart pitcher. Stir until corn syrup dissolves. (Stir in additional corn syrup to taste.) Refrigerate 2 hours or until cold. Stir in ginger ale just before serving.

Divide frozen fruit between 8 (12-ounce) glasses or 10 wide-rimmed wine glasses. Fill glasses with punch. Garnish with mint springs, if desired. Serve immediately. *Makes 8 to 10 servings (about 5 cups)*

Banana Smoothies & Pops

1 (14-ounce) can EAGLE® BRAND Sweetened Condensed Milk (NOT evaporated milk)
1 (8-ounce) container vanilla yogurt
2 ripe bananas
$\frac{1}{2}$ cup orange juice

1. In blender container, combine all ingredients; blend until smooth. Stop occasionally to scrape down sides.
2. Serve immediately. Store leftovers covered in refrigerator.

Makes 4 cups

Banana Smoothie Pops: Spoon banana mixture into 8 (5-ounce) paper cups. Freeze 30 minutes. Insert wooden craft sticks into the center of each cup; freeze until firm. Makes 8 pops.

Fruit Smoothies: Substitute 1 cup of your favorite fruit and $\frac{1}{2}$ cup any fruit juice for bananas and orange juice.

Prep Time: 5 minutes

"Moo-vin" Vanilla Milk Shakes

1 pint low-fat sugar-free vanilla ice cream
$\frac{1}{2}$ cup fat-free (skim) milk
$\frac{1}{2}$ teaspoon vanilla
$\frac{1}{8}$ teaspoon decorator sprinkles (optional)

Combine all ingredients except decorator sprinkles in blender container. Cover and blend until smooth. Pour into 2 small glasses. Add decorator sprinkles, if desired. Serve immediately.

Makes 2 servings

Bobbing Head Punch

Assorted candies
Assorted fruit slices and pieces
Water
6 cups white grape juice
2 cups apple juice or 2 additional cups ginger ale
4 cups ginger ale
Green food coloring

1. Arrange candies and fruit pieces in bottom of 9-inch glass pie plate to create a face. (Remember, the bottom of the face is what will show in the punch bowl.)

2. Add water to cover face and carefully place in freezer. Freeze overnight.

3. At time of serving, add juice and ginger ale to 4- to 5-quart punch bowl. Tint mixture green. Invert pie plate, placing one hand underneath, and run under cold running water to release frozen face. Place ice mold upside down on top of juice mixture and serve.   *Makes 20 cups*

Plum Slush

6 fresh California plums, halved, pitted and coarsely chopped
1 can (6 ounces) frozen cranberry juice concentrate
20 ice cubes, cracked

Add plums, juice concentrate and ice cubes to food processor or blender. Process until smooth. Serve immediately.   *Makes 8 servings*

Favorite recipe from **California Tree Fruit Agreement**

Fat-Free Honey Berry Milkshakes

2½ cups strawberries or assorted berries
1 pint nonfat vanilla frozen yogurt or ice cream
½ cup nonfat milk
¼ cup honey
4 small mint sprigs

Combine all ingredients except mint sprigs in blender or food processor; process about 30 seconds or until smooth. Pour into tall glasses. Garnish with mint sprigs. *Makes 4 cups*

Favorite recipe from **National Honey Board**

Cookie Milk Shakes

1 pint vanilla ice cream
4 chocolate sandwich cookies or chocolate-covered graham crackers

Scoop ice cream into blender fitted with metal blade. Crush cookies in resealable plastic food storage bag with rolling pin or in food processor. Place cookies in blender. Process until well-combined. Pour into 2 glasses. Serve immediately. *Makes 2 milk shakes*

Nectarine Mocktail

3 fresh California nectarines, halved, pitted and diced

1 container (10 ounces) unsweetened frozen strawberries,
  partially thawed

1 bottle (28 ounces) club soda or sugar-free ginger ale

8 mint sprigs (optional)

Add nectarines, strawberries and 1 cup club soda to blender. Process until smooth. Pour into chilled glasses about ⅔ full. Top with remaining club soda. Garnish with mint, if desired. *Makes 8 servings*

Favorite recipe from **California Tree Fruit Agreement**

"Moo-vin" Strawberry Milk Shakes

1 pint low-fat sugar-free vanilla ice cream

1 cup thawed frozen unsweetened strawberries

¼ cup fat-free (skim) milk

¼ teaspoon vanilla

Combine all ingredients in blender container. Cover and blend until smooth. Pour into 2 small glasses. Serve immediately.

Makes 2 servings

Purple Cow Jumped Over the Moon

3 cups vanilla nonfat frozen yogurt

I cup reduced-fat (2%) milk

½ cup thawed frozen grape juice concentrate (undiluted)

1½ teaspoons lemon juice

Place yogurt, milk, grape juice concentrate and lemon juice in food processor or blender container; process until smooth. Serve immediately.

Makes 8 (½-cup) servings

Razzmatazz Shake: Place I quart vanilla nonfat frozen yogurt, I cup vanilla nonfat yogurt and ¼ cup chocolate nonfat syrup in food processor or blender container; process until smooth. Pour ½ of mixture evenly into 12 glasses; top with ½ of (12-ounce) can root beer. Fill glasses equally with remaining yogurt mixture; top with remaining root beer. Makes 12 (⅔-cup) servings.

Sunshine Shake: Place I quart vanilla nonfat frozen yogurt, 1⅓ cups orange juice, I cup fresh or thawed frozen raspberries and I teaspoon sugar in food processor or blender container; process until smooth. Pour into 10 glasses; sprinkle with ground nutmeg. Makes 10 (½-cup) servings.

Fruit 'n Juice Breakfast Shake

I extra-ripe, medium DOLE® Banana

¾ cup DOLE® Pineapple Juice

½ cup lowfat vanilla yogurt

½ cup blueberries

Combine all ingredients in blender. Blend until smooth.

Makes 2 servings

128

Super Cherry Cola Floats

1 cup boiling water

1 package (4-serving size) JELL-O® Brand Cherry Flavor
Gelatin

1¼ cups cold cola

1 pint vanilla ice cream (2 cups)

STIR boiling water into gelatin in medium bowl 2 minutes until completely dissolved. Stir in cola. Refrigerate 20 to 30 minutes or until slightly thickened (consistency of unbeaten egg whites). Reserve ½ cup gelatin.

PLACE ½ cup ice cream into each of 4 tall ice cream soda glasses. Top with thickened gelatin mixture.

BEAT reserved ½ cup gelatin mixture with electric mixer on medium speed until light and fluffy. Spoon into each glass.

REFRIGERATE 2 hours or until firm.   *Makes 4 servings*

Special Extra: Garnish each float with a maraschino cherry and sprinkles.

Prep Time: 15 minutes plus refrigerating

Peanut Butter-Banana Shake

1 ripe banana, cut into chunks

2 tablespoons peanut butter

½ cup vanilla ice cream

1 cup milk

Place all ingredients in blender container. Cover; process until smooth.

Makes about 2 cups

Triple Delicious Hot Chocolate

⅓ cup sugar

¼ cup unsweetened cocoa powder

¼ teaspoon salt

3 cups milk, divided

¾ teaspoon vanilla

1 cup heavy cream

1 square (1 ounce) bittersweet chocolate

1 square (1 ounce) white chocolate

¾ cup whipped cream

6 teaspoons mini chocolate chips or shaved bittersweet chocolate

Slow Cooker Directions

1. Combine sugar, cocoa, salt and ½ cup milk in medium bowl. Beat until smooth. Pour into slow cooker. Add remaining 2½ cups milk and vanilla. Cover; cook on LOW 2 hours.

2. Add cream. Cover and cook on LOW 10 minutes. Stir in bittersweet and white chocolates until melted.

3. Pour hot chocolate into 6 coffee cups. Top each with 2 tablespoons whipped cream and 1 teaspoon chocolate chips.   *Makes 6 servings*

Shamrock Smoothies

1 tablespoon sugar

2 green spearmint candy leaves

2 thin round chocolate mints or chocolate sandwich cookies

1 ripe banana, peeled and cut into chunks

1 cup ice cubes

¾ cup apple juice

¼ cup plain yogurt

½ teaspoon vanilla

¼ teaspoon orange extract

2 or 3 drops green food color

1. Place small sheet of waxed paper on work surface; sprinkle with sugar. Place spearmint leaves on waxed paper; top with second sheet of waxed paper. Roll out leaves to ¼-inch thickness. Cut out 2 (1¼×1-inch) shamrock shapes using small knife or scissors. Press 1 shamrock onto each mint; set aside.

2. Place banana, ice cubes, apple juice, yogurt, vanilla, orange extract and food color in blender or food processor; blend until smooth and frothy. Pour into glasses. Garnish with mints.

Makes 2 servings (about 8 ounces each)

Sinister Slushies

4 bottles brightly colored sport drinks
4 to 8 ice cube trays
Resealable plastic freezer storage bags

1. Pour sport drinks into separate ice cube trays and freeze overnight.

2. Just before serving, pop frozen cubes into plastic bags, one color at a time. Seal bag and smash cubes with rolling pin.

3. Layer different colored ice slush in clear glasses to make wild combinations. Serve with straws. *Makes 4 to 8 servings*

Mysterious Chocolate Mint Cooler

2 cups cold whole milk or half-and-half
¼ cup chocolate syrup
1 teaspoon peppermint extract
Crushed ice
Aerosol whipped topping
Mint leaves

Combine first 3 ingredients in small pitcher; stir until well blended. Fill glasses with crushed ice. Pour chocolate mint mixture over ice. Top with whipped topping and garnish with mint leaves.

Makes about 2 (10-ounce) servings

Snowbird Mocktails

3 cups pineapple juice

1 can (14 ounces) sweetened condensed milk

1 can (6 ounces) frozen orange juice concentrate, thawed

½ teaspoon coconut extract

1 bottle (32 ounces) ginger ale, chilled

1. Combine pineapple juice, sweetened condensed milk, orange juice concentrate and coconut extract in large pitcher; stir well. Refrigerate, covered, up to 1 week.

2. To serve, pour ½ cup pineapple juice mixture into individual glasses (over crushed ice, if desired). Top off each glass with about ⅓ cup ginger ale.   *Makes 10 servings*

Prep Time: 10 minutes

Super Suggestion!

Store unopened cans of sweetened
condensed milk at room temperature
up to 6 months. Once opened,
store in airtight container in
refrigerator for up to 5 days.

Easy Pudding Milk Shake

3 cups cold milk

1 package (4-serving size) JELL-O® Instant Pudding & Pie
   Filling, any flavor

1½ cups ice cream, any flavor

POUR milk into blender container. Add pudding mix and ice cream;
cover. Blend on high speed 30 seconds or until smooth. Pour into glasses
and garnish as desired. Serve immediately.   *Makes 5 servings*

Prep Time: 5 minutes

Quick Apple Punch

4 cups MOTT'S® Apple Juice

2 cups cranberry juice cocktail

2 tablespoons lemon juice

1 liter ginger ale, chilled

Crushed ice, as needed

In large bowl, combine apple juice, cranberry juice and lemon juice.
Fifteen minutes before serving, add ginger ale and crushed ice. Do not
stir.   *Makes 15 servings*

● ● ● ● ● ● ● ● ● ● ● ● ●

**What did the banana do when
it heard the ice scream?**

● ● ● ● ● ● ● ● ● ● ● ● ●

Answer: It split!

Monkey Shake

2 cups cold milk

I ripe banana

I package (4-serving size) JELL-O® Chocolate Flavor Instant Pudding & Pie Filling

2 cups crushed ice

POUR milk into blender container. Add banana, pudding mix and ice; cover. Blend on high speed 15 seconds or until smooth. Serve at once.

Makes 4 servings

How To: Mixture will thicken as it stands. To thin, just add more milk, ¼ cup at a time for desired thickness.

Great Substitute: Try using JELL-O® White Chocolate Flavor Instant Pudding instead of Chocolate Flavor.

Prep Time: 10 minutes

Raspberry-Lemon Smoothie

I cup frozen raspberries

I carton (8 ounces) lemon-flavored yogurt

½ cup milk

I teaspoon vanilla

Place all ingredients in blender. Cover; blend until smooth.

Makes about 1½ cups

Super Suggestion!

Serve the Raspberry-Lemon Smoothie on a hot summer day for a refreshing treat!

"Moo-vin" Chocolate-Cherry Milk Shakes

   1 pint low-fat sugar-free chocolate ice cream
   ¾ cup drained canned pitted tart red cherries
   ¼ cup fat-free (skim) milk
   ¼ teaspoon vanilla
   ⅛ teaspoon decorator sprinkles (optional)

Combine all ingredients except decorator sprinkles in blender container. Cover and blend until smooth. Pour into 2 small glasses. Add decorator sprinkles, if desired. Serve immediately.   *Makes 2 servings*

Strawberry Lemonade

   1 cup fresh strawberries, quartered
   1 cup fresh lemon juice (from about 4 lemons)
   ¾ cup sucralose, granular form*
   4 cups water

Sold as SPLENDA®

1. Place strawberries in food processor or blender; process until smooth. Pour into large pitcher.

2. Add lemon juice to pitcher along with sucralose and water. Stir.

3. Strain strawberry seeds and pulp, if desired, by pouring lemonade through strainer.

4. Serve in tall glasses filled with ice.   *Makes 4 servings*

Pizza Fondue

½ pound bulk Italian sausage

1 cup chopped onion

2 jars (26 ounces each) meatless pasta sauce

4 ounces thinly sliced ham, finely chopped

1 package (3 ounces) sliced pepperoni, finely chopped

¼ teaspoon red pepper flakes

1 pound mozzarella cheese, cut into ¾-inch cubes

1 loaf Italian or French bread, cut into 1-inch cubes

Slow Cooker Directions

1. Cook sausage and onion in large skillet until sausage is browned. Drain off fat.

2. Transfer sausage mixture to slow cooker. Stir in pasta sauce, ham, pepperoni and pepper flakes. Cover; cook on LOW 3 to 4 hours.

3. Serve sauce with cheese cubes, bread cubes and fondue forks.

Makes 20 to 25 appetizer servings

Prep Time: 15 minutes
Cook Time: 3 to 4 hours

Corn Dogs

8 hot dogs

8 wooden craft sticks

1 package (about 16 ounces) refrigerated grand-size corn biscuits

⅓ cup *French's*® Classic Yellow® Mustard

8 slices American cheese, cut in half

1. Preheat oven to 350°F. Insert 1 wooden craft stick halfway into each hot dog; set aside.

2. Separate biscuits. On floured board, press or roll each biscuit into a 7×4-inch oval. Spread *2 teaspoons* mustard lengthwise down center of each biscuit. Top each with 2 pieces of cheese. Place hot dog in center of biscuit. Fold top of dough over end of hot dog. Fold sides towards center enclosing hot dog. Pinch edges to seal.

3. Place corn dogs, seam-side down, on greased baking sheet. Bake 20 to 25 minutes or until golden brown. Cool slightly before serving.

Makes 8 servings

Tip: Corn dogs may be made without wooden craft sticks.

Prep Time: 15 minutes
Cook Time: 20 minutes

Cartoona Sandwiches

½ cup low fat mayonnaise

½ cup plain low fat yogurt

1½ teaspoons curry powder (optional)

1 cup **SUN-MAID®** Raisins or Fruit Bits

½ cup diced celery, or red or green bell pepper

1 green onion thinly sliced

1 large can (12 ounces) tuna packed in water, or substitute 1¼ cups chopped cooked chicken (two small chicken breasts)

6 sandwich rolls, round or oblong shaped

1. **MAKE FILLING:** Mix in a medium bowl, the mayonnaise, yogurt, curry powder, if desired, Sun-Maid® Raisins or Fruit Bits, celery or bell pepper, and green onion. Stir in tuna or chicken.

2. **MAKE "CAR":** Cut* a ½-inch slice off the top of a roll. With fingers or a fork, scoop out bread from center of roll.

3. **ATTACH** Sun-Maid® Apricots, carrot slices or other round ingredient to a toothpick to make car "wheels." Insert wheels into bottom edge of roll. Add apple slices for "fenders," if desired.

4. **MAKE** "headlights" using toothpicks to attach raisins on one end of the roll. Cut "doors" in sides of roll, if desired.

5. **FILL** roll with about ½ cup tuna or chicken salad. Place roll top on top of "car." Repeat with remaining rolls. Remove all toothpicks before eating.   *Makes 6 sandwiches*

*Adult supervision is suggested.

Prep Time: 20 minutes

Chicken Dogs on a Stick

  1 tube (8 ounces) refrigerated crescent dinner rolls (8 rolls)
  1 pound boneless skinless chicken breast halves
  3 tablespoons **CRISCO® Oil***
  ¾ cup shredded Romano cheese
  1 package (3 ounces) cream cheese, softened
  ¼ cup chopped onion
  3 tablespoons grated Parmesan cheese
  ¼ teaspoon Italian seasoning
  ¼ teaspoon pepper
  8 frozen treat sticks

Use your favorite Crisco Oil product.

Heat oven to 375°F.

Separate roll dough into triangles. Stretch each triangle into rectangle about 4 inches long.

Rinse chicken; pat dry. Cut into small cubes. Heat oil in medium skillet on high heat. Add chicken. Stir-fry about 3 minutes or until no longer pink in center. Drain. Cool.

Combine Romano cheese, cream cheese, onion, Parmesan cheese, Italian seasoning, pepper and chicken in medium bowl. Mix well. Spoon about ⅓ cup filling onto each dough rectangle. Wrap around wooden stick so that one end of stick can be used as "handle." Press and pinch dough ends to seal. Place on baking sheet.

Bake for 15 to 20 minutes or until browned. Cool on rack 5 to 10 minutes before serving. *Makes 8 servings*

Pizza Rollers

1 package (10 ounces) refrigerated pizza dough
½ cup pizza sauce
18 slices turkey pepperoni
6 sticks mozzarella cheese

1. Preheat oven to 425°F. Coat baking sheet with nonstick cooking spray.

2. Roll out pizza dough on baking sheet to form 12×9-inch rectangle. Cut pizza dough into 6 (4½×4-inch) rectangles. Spread about 1 tablespoon sauce over center third of each rectangle. Top with 3 slices pepperoni and stick of mozzarella cheese. Bring ends of dough together over cheese, pinching to seal. Place seam side down on prepared baking sheet.

3. Bake in center of oven 10 minutes or until golden brown.

Makes 6 servings

Tortellini Teasers

½ (9-ounce) package refrigerated cheese tortellini
1 large red or green bell pepper, cut into 1-inch pieces
2 medium carrots, peeled and sliced ½ inch thick
1 medium zucchini, sliced ½ inch thick
12 medium fresh mushrooms
12 cherry tomatoes
1 can (15 ounces) tomato sauce

1. Cook tortellini according to package directions; drain.

2. Alternate 1 tortellini and 2 to 3 vegetable pieces on long frilled wooden picks or wooden skewers.

3. Warm tomato sauce in small saucepan. Serve with dippers.

Makes 6 servings

Pizza Rollers

Baseball Sandwich

Ingredients

1 (1-pound) round sourdough or white bread loaf

2 cups mayonnaise or salad dressing, divided

¼ pound thinly sliced roast beef

1 slice (about 1 ounce) provolone or Swiss cheese

3 tablespoons roasted red peppers, well drained

3 tablespoons spicy mustard, divided

¼ pound thinly sliced ham

1 slice (about 1 ounce) Cheddar cheese

3 tablespoons dill pickle slices

2 tablespoons thinly sliced onion

Red food color

Supplies

Pastry bag and small writing tip

1. Cut thin slice off top of bread loaf; set aside. With serrated knife, cut around sides of bread, leaving ¼-inch-thick bread shell. Lift out center portion of bread; horizontally cut removed bread round into 3 slices of equal thickness.

2. Spread 1 tablespoon mayonnaise onto bottom of hollowed out loaf; top with layers of roast beef and provolone cheese. Cover with bottom bread slice and red peppers.

3. Spread top of middle bread slice with ½ of mustard; place over peppers. Top with layers of ham and Cheddar cheese. Spread remaining bread slice with remaining mustard; place over ham and Cheddar cheese. Top with pickles and onion. Replace top of bread loaf.

4. Reserve ⅓ cup mayonnaise; set aside. Frost outside of entire loaf of bread with remaining mayonnaise. Color reserved ⅓ cup mayonnaise with red food color; spoon into pastry bag fitted with writing tip. Pipe red mayonnaise onto bread to resemble stitches on baseball.

Makes 6 to 8 servings

Perfect Pita Pizzas

2 whole wheat or white pita bread rounds
½ **cup spaghetti or pizza sauce**
¾ **cup (3 ounces) shredded part-skim mozzarella cheese**
1 small zucchini, sliced ¼ inch thick
½ **small carrot, peeled and sliced**
2 cherry tomatoes, halved
¼ **small green bell pepper, sliced**

1. Preheat oven to 375°F. Line baking sheet with foil; set aside.

2. Using small scissors, carefully split each pita bread round around edge; separate to form 2 rounds.

3. Place rounds, rough sides up, on prepared baking sheet. Bake 5 minutes.

4. Spread 2 tablespoons spaghetti sauce onto each round; sprinkle with cheese. Decorate with vegetables to create faces. Bake 10 to 12 minutes or until cheese melts.   *Makes 4 servings*

Pepperoni Pita Pizzas: Prepare pita rounds, partially bake and top with spaghetti sauce and cheese as directed. Place 2 small pepperoni slices on each pizza for eyes. Decorate with cut-up fresh vegetables for rest of face. Continue to bake as directed.

● ● ● ● ● ● ● ● ● ● ●
Why does a Mexican weather report make you hungry?
● ● ● ● ● ● ● ● ● ● ●

Answer: Because it's chili today and hot tamale!

Sea Serpents

1 package crescent dinner rolls (8 rolls)
Fruit-flavored cereal rings
1 egg, beaten
Sunflower seeds, sesame seeds or poppy seeds
1 can (6 ounces) water-packed tuna, drained
Mayonnaise
Parsley and pimiento strips (optional)

1. Separate dough into triangles. Press each triangle into serpent shape, with thin tapered tail and wider head, on baking sheet. Head should be about ¼-inch thick.

2. Press cereal rings onto head for eyes. Brush dough serpents with egg and sprinkle with choice of seeds. Bake according to package directions.

3. When cooled, slice head end lengthwise to form a mouth. Mix tuna with mayonnaise to taste and fill mouth with tuna mixture. Add sprigs of parsley for seaweed and pimiento strips for tongues, if desired.

Makes 8 servings

Super Suggestion!

If your kids don't eat tuna, fill the mouths of these hungry creatures with peanut butter, egg salad, chicken salad, or even their favorite cold cuts cut into strips.

Chili Dogs

½ pound lean ground beef

1 cup chopped onions

1 can (6 ounces) HUNT'S® Tomato Paste No Salt Added

1 cup water

2 tablespoons GEBHARDT® Chili Powder

1 tablespoon prepared yellow mustard

½ teaspoon garlic powder

½ teaspoon ground cumin

¼ teaspoon sugar

⅛ teaspoon crushed red pepper

1 pound BUTTERBALL® Turkey Franks

10 hot dog buns

In skillet, brown beef and onions. Stir in tomato paste, water, chili powder, mustard, garlic powder, cumin, sugar and crushed red pepper; heat through. Meanwhile, heat or grill hot dogs. To serve, place hot dogs in buns; spoon chili down center of each.   *Makes 10 chili dogs*

Pizza Snack Cups

1 can (12 ounces) refrigerated biscuits (10 biscuits)

½ pound ground beef

1 jar (14 ounces) RAGÚ® Pizza Quick® Sauce

½ cup shredded mozzarella cheese (about 2 ounces)

1. Preheat oven to 375°F. In 12-cup muffin pan, evenly press each biscuit in bottom and up side of each cup; chill until ready to fill.

2. In 10-inch skillet, brown ground beef over medium-high heat; drain. Stir in Ragú Pizza Quick Sauce and heat through.

3. Evenly spoon beef mixture into prepared muffin cups. Bake 15 minutes. Sprinkle with cheese and bake an additional 5 minutes or until cheese is melted and biscuits are golden. Let stand 5 minutes. Gently remove pizza cups from muffin pan and serve.

155

Makes 10 pizza cups

Surprise Package Cupcakes

1 package (18 ounces) chocolate cake mix, plus ingredients
to prepare mix

Food coloring (optional)

1 can (16 ounces) vanilla frosting

1 tube (4¼ ounces) white decorator icing

72 chewy fruit squares, assorted colors

Assorted round sprinkles and birthday candles

1. Line standard (2½-inch) muffin cups with paper liners, or spray with nonstick cooking spray. Prepare cake and bake in muffin cups according to directions. Cool in pans on wire racks 15 minutes. Remove cupcakes and cool completely.

2. If desired, tint frosting with food coloring, adding a few drops at a time until desired color is reached. Frost cupcakes with white or tinted frosting.

3. Use decorator icing to pipe "ribbons" on fruit squares to resemble wrapped presents. Place 3 candy presents on each cupcake. Decorate with sprinkles and candles as desired. *Makes 24 cupcakes*

S'Mores on a Stick

1 (14-ounce) can **EAGLE® BRAND** Sweetened Condensed Milk (**NOT** evaporated milk), divided

1½ cups milk chocolate mini chips, divided

1 cup miniature marshmallows

11 whole graham crackers, halved crosswise

Toppings: chopped peanuts, mini candy-coated chocolate pieces, sprinkles

1. Microwave half of Eagle Brand in microwave-safe bowl at HIGH (100% power) 1½ minutes. Stir in 1 cup chips until smooth; stir in marshmallows.

2. Spread evenly by heaping tablespoonfuls onto 11 graham cracker halves. Top with remaining graham cracker halves; place on waxed paper.

3. Microwave remaining Eagle Brand at HIGH (100% power) 1½ minutes; stir in remaining ½ cup chips, stirring until smooth. Drizzle mixture over cookies and sprinkle with desired toppings.

4. Let stand for 2 hours; insert a wooden craft stick into center of each cookie.   *Makes 11 servings*

Prep Time: 10 minutes
Cook Time: 3 minutes

Chocolate Chip Applesauce Snacking Cake

1⅓ cups all-purpose flour

1 cup granulated sugar

¾ teaspoon baking soda

¾ teaspoon salt

½ teaspoon ground cinnamon

¼ teaspoon baking powder

¼ teaspoon ground allspice

½ cup shortening

1 cup chunky applesauce

2 eggs

1 teaspoon vanilla extract

½ cup chopped pecans

½ cup HERSHEY'S Semi-Sweet Chocolate Chips

Powdered sugar (optional)

Vanilla Frosting (optional, recipe page 162)

Chocolate Drizzle (optional, recipe page 162)

1. Heat oven to 350°F. Grease and flour 9-inch square baking pan.

2. Combine flour, granulated sugar, baking soda, salt, cinnamon, baking powder and allspice in large bowl. Add shortening, applesauce, eggs and vanilla. Beat on low speed of mixer to combine; beat on medium speed 1 minute or until ingredients are well blended. Stir in pecans and chocolate chips; pour into prepared pan.

3. Bake 40 to 45 minutes or until wooden pick inserted in center comes out clean. Cool in pan on wire rack. Sprinkle with powdered sugar or spread Vanilla Frosting, if desired, on cake. Prepare Chocolate Drizzle, if desired; drizzle over top of Vanilla Frosting.

Makes 16 servings

continued on page 162

Chocolate Chip Applesauce Snacking Cake, continued

Vanilla Frosting: Beat 3 tablespoons softened butter or margarine in small bowl until fluffy. Add 1½ cups powdered sugar and ½ teaspoon vanilla extract alternately with 1 to 2 tablespoons milk, beating to spreading consistency. Makes about 1 cup frosting.

Chocolate Drizzle: Place ½ cup HERSHEY'S Semi-Sweet Chocolate Chips and 1 tablespoon shortening (do not use butter, margarine, spread or oil) in small microwave-safe bowl. Microwave at HIGH (100%) 30 seconds; stir. If necessary, microwave an additional 15 seconds or just until chips are melted and mixture is smooth when stirred.

Wild Side Sundaes

> **4 packages (4-serving size) JELL-O® Brand Gelatin, 4 different flavors**
>
> **4 cups boiling water**
>
> **2 cups cold water**
>
> **1 tub (8 ounces) COOL WHIP® Whipped Topping, thawed**
> **Additional thawed COOL WHIP® Whipped Topping**

DISSOLVE each package of gelatin completely in 1 cup boiling water in separate bowls. Stir ½ cup cold water into each bowl of gelatin. Pour each mixture into separate 8-inch square pans. Refrigerate at least 3 hours or until firm. Cut gelatin in each pan into ½-inch cubes.

LAYER gelatin cubes alternately with whipped topping in sundae glasses. Garnish with dollop of additional whipped topping.

REFRIGERATE until ready to serve. *Makes 16 servings*

Banana Split Cupcakes

1 package (about 18 ounces) yellow cake mix, divided

1 cup water

1 cup mashed ripe bananas

3 eggs

1 cup chopped drained maraschino cherries

1½ cups miniature semi-sweet chocolate chips, divided

1½ cups prepared vanilla frosting

1 cup marshmallow creme

1 teaspoon shortening

30 whole maraschino cherries, drained and patted dry

1. Preheat oven to 350°F. Line 30 standard (2½-inch) muffin cups with paper liners.

2. Reserve 2 tablespoons cake mix. Combine remaining cake mix, water, bananas and eggs in large bowl. Beat at low speed of electric mixer until moistened, about 30 seconds. Beat at medium speed 2 minutes. Combine chopped cherries and reserved cake mix in small bowl. Stir chopped cherry mixture and 1 cup chocolate chips into batter.

3. Spoon batter into prepared muffin cups. Bake 15 to 20 minutes or until toothpick inserted into centers comes out clean. Cool in pans on wire racks 10 minutes. Remove to wire racks; cool completely.

4. Combine frosting and marshmallow creme in medium bowl until well blended. Frost each cupcake with frosting mixture.

5. Combine remaining ½ cup chocolate chips and shortening in small microwavable bowl. Microwave at HIGH 30 to 45 seconds, stirring after 30 seconds, or until smooth. Drizzle chocolate mixture over cupcakes. Place one whole cherry on each cupcake.   *Makes 30 cupcakes*

Note: If desired, omit chocolate drizzle and top cupcakes with colored sprinkles.

Lazy Daisy Cupcakes

1 package (18 ounces) yellow cake mix, plus ingredients to
   prepare mix
Food coloring
1 can (16 ounces) vanilla frosting
30 large marshmallows
24 small round candies or gum drops

1. Line standard (2½-inch) muffin cups with paper liners, or spray with nonstick cooking spray. Prepare cake and bake in muffin cups according to directions. Cool in pans on wire racks 15 minutes. Remove cupcakes and cool completely.

2. Add food coloring to frosting, a few drops at a time, until desired color is reached. Frost cooled cupcakes with tinted frosting.

3. With scissors, cut each marshmallow crosswise into 4 pieces. Stretch pieces into petal shapes and place 5 pieces on each cupcake to form a flower. Place candy in center of each flower.   *Makes 24 cupcakes*

● ● ● ● ● ● ● ● ● ● ● ●

Why did the strawberry need a lawyer?

● ● ● ● ● ● ● ● ● ● ● ●

Answer: Because it was in a jam!

164

Cool Candy Cones

6 flat-bottom ice cream cones

1 tub (8 ounces) COOL WHIP® Whipped Topping, thawed

⅓ cup multicolored sprinkles

1 cup chopped candy bars (chocolate-covered wafer bars, peanut butter cups, etc.)

SPREAD top rims of ice cream cones with whipped topping. Roll in sprinkles.

STIR candy into remaining topping. Carefully spoon into prepared ice cream cones. Garnish tops with additional chopped candy and sprinkles, if desired. Serve immediately, or refrigerate or freeze until ready to serve. *Makes 6 servings*

Berries and Cream: Substitute 1 cup raspberries or chopped strawberries for the chopped candy bars.

Prep Time: 10 minutes

Aquarium Cups

¾ cup boiling water

1 package (4-serving size) JELL-O® Brand Berry Blue Flavor Gelatin Dessert

½ cup cold water

Ice cubes

Gummy fish

STIR boiling water into gelatin in medium bowl at least 2 minutes until completely dissolved. Mix cold water and ice cubes to make 1¼ cups. Add to gelatin, stirring until slightly thickened. Remove any remaining ice. (If mixture is still thin, refrigerate until slightly thickened.)

POUR thickened gelatin into 4 dessert dishes. Suspend gummy fish in gelatin. Refrigerate 1 hour or until firm. *Makes 4 servings*

Prep Time: 10 minutes
Chill Time: 1 hour

Cool Candy Cones

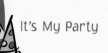

Colorific Pizza Cookie

   1 package (17½ ounces) sugar cookie mix
   ⅔ cup mini candy-coated chocolate pieces
   ⅓ cup powdered sugar
   2 to 3 teaspoons milk

Preheat oven to 375°F.

Prepare cookie mix according to package directions. Spread into ungreased 12-inch pizza pan. Sprinkle evenly with chocolate pieces; press gently into dough.

Bake 20 to 24 minutes or until lightly browned. Cool 2 minutes in pan. Transfer to wire rack and cool completely.

Blend powdered sugar and milk until smooth, adding enough milk to reach drizzling consistency. Drizzle icing over cooled pizza cookie with spoon or fork. Cut into wedges.

Makes 12 servings

Hershey's Syrup Snacking Brownies

   ½ cup (1 stick) butter or margarine, softened
   1 cup sugar
   1½ cups (16-ounce can) HERSHEY'S Syrup
   4 eggs
   1¼ cups all-purpose flour
   1 cup HERSHEY'S Semi-Sweet Chocolate Chips

1. Heat oven to 350°F. Grease 13×9×2-inch baking pan.

2. Beat butter and sugar in large bowl. Add syrup, eggs and flour; beat well. Stir in chocolate chips. Pour batter into prepared pan.

3. Bake 30 to 35 minutes or until brownies begin to pull away from sides of pan. Cool completely in pan on wire rack. Cut into bars.

Makes about 36 brownies

Cookies & Cream Cupcakes

2¼ cups all-purpose flour

1 tablespoon baking powder

½ teaspoon salt

1⅔ cups sugar

½ cup (1 stick) butter, softened

1 cup milk

2 teaspoons vanilla

3 egg whites

1 cup crushed chocolate sandwich cookies (about 10 cookies) plus additional for garnish

1 container (16 ounces) vanilla frosting

1. Preheat oven to 350°F. Line 24 standard (2½-inch) muffin pan cups with paper liners.

2. Sift flour, baking powder and salt together in large bowl. Stir in sugar. Add butter, milk and vanilla; beat with electric mixer at low speed 30 seconds. Beat at medium speed 2 minutes. Add egg whites; beat 2 minutes. Stir in 1 cup crushed cookies.

3. Spoon batter into prepared muffin pans. Bake 20 to 25 minutes or until toothpick inserted into centers comes out clean. Cool in pans on wire racks 10 minutes. Remove to racks; cool completely.

4. Frost cupcakes; garnish with additional crushed cookies.

Makes 24 cupcakes

Chocolate Peanut Butter Fondue

⅓ **cup sugar**

⅓ **cup unsweetened cocoa powder**

⅓ **cup low-fat (1%) milk**

 3 **tablespoons light corn syrup**

 2 **tablespoons reduced-fat peanut butter**

½ **teaspoon vanilla**

 2 **medium bananas, cut into 1-inch pieces**

16 **large strawberries**

 2 **medium apples, cored and sliced**

1. Mix sugar, cocoa, milk, corn syrup and peanut butter in medium saucepan. Cook over medium heat, stirring constantly, until hot. Remove from heat; stir in vanilla.

2. Pour fondue into medium serving bowl; serve warm or at room temperature with fruit for dipping. *Makes 8 servings*

● ● ● ● ● ● ● ● ● ● ●

**What did the computer
order at the restaurant?**

● ● ● ● ● ● ● ● ● ● ●

Answer: A byte!

Magical Wizard Hats

1 package (18 ounces) cake mix, any flavor, plus ingredients
  to prepare mix
2 cans (16 ounces each) vanilla frosting
  Assorted food coloring
2 packages (4 ounces each) sugar cones
  Assorted sprinkles, silver dragées and colored sugar
1 tube (0.6 ounce) black piping gel

1. Line standard (2½-inch) muffin cups with paper liners, or spray with
nonstick cooking spray. Prepare cake and bake in muffin cups according
to directions. Cool in pans on wire racks 15 minutes. Remove cupcakes
and cool completely.

2. Frost cupcakes and set aside. Separate ½ cup remaining frosting into
small bowl and tint yellow, or desired color. Tint remaining frosting
purple, or desired color.

3. Spread each sugar cone with purple frosting, covering completely.
Place 1 cone upside down on each frosted cupcake. Spoon yellow
frosting into small resealable plastic food storage bag. With scissors, snip
off 1 corner of bag. Gently squeeze bag to pipe yellow frosting around
base of each frosted cone. Add sprinkles and decorate cones as desired
with black piping gel and assorted decorations.   *Makes 24 cupcakes*

Jack-O-Lantern Snacks

8 ounces cream cheese, softened
Red and yellow food coloring
8 large slices dark pumpernickel bread
1 small green bell pepper
Sliced Genoa salami

1. Place cream cheese in small bowl. Add 8 drops red and 6 drops yellow food coloring to turn cream cheese orange. Mix well and adjust color as desired.

2. Toast bread and allow to cool. Using large pumpkin cookie cutter or metal 1-cup measure, cut round shape from each slice of toast leaving "stem" on top. Spread cream cheese over toast all the way to edges. Cut "stems" from green pepper and place over stem on toast. Cut triangle "eyes" and mouth with several "teeth" from sliced salami. Arrange over each pumpkin toast. *Makes 8 servings*

Dainty Digits

2 tablespoons cream cheese
24 baby carrots
24 almond slices
Salsa

Spread small dab of cream cheese on tip of each baby carrot. Gently press almond slice onto cream cheese to resemble fingernails. Serve on platter with bowl of salsa for dipping. *Makes 4 servings*

Jack-O-Lantern Snacks

Graveyard Treat

2¼ cups chocolate wafer cookie crumbs, divided

½ cup sugar, divided

½ cup (1 stick) margarine or butter, melted

1 package (8 ounces) PHILADELPHIA® Cream Cheese,
    cubed, softened

1 tub (12 ounces) COOL WHIP® Whipped Topping, thawed

2 cups boiling water

1 package (8-serving size) or 2 packages (4-serving size)
    JELL-O® Brand Orange Flavor Gelatin Dessert

½ cup cold water

Ice cubes

Rectangular or oval-shaped sandwich cookies

Decorator icings

Candy corn and pumpkins

MIX 2 cups of the cookie crumbs, ¼ cup of the sugar and the melted margarine with fork in 13×9-inch baking pan until crumbs are well moistened. Press firmly onto bottom of pan to form crust. Refrigerate.

BEAT cream cheese and remaining ¼ cup sugar in medium bowl with wire whisk until smooth. Gently stir in ½ of the whipped topping. Spread evenly over crust.

STIR boiling water into gelatin in medium bowl 2 minutes or until completely dissolved. Mix cold water and ice cubes to make 1½ cups. Add to gelatin; stir until slightly thickened (consistency of unbeaten egg whites). Remove any remaining ice. Spoon gelatin over cream cheese layer.

REFRIGERATE 3 hours or until firm. Spread remaining whipped topping over gelatin just before serving; sprinkle with remaining ¼ cup cookie crumbs. Decorate sandwich cookies with icings to make "tombstones." Stand tombstones on top of dessert with candies to resemble a graveyard. Cut into squares to serve.

Makes 15 to 18 servings

Trick or Treats

Trick-or-Treat Pizza Biscuits

1 can (16 to 17 ounces or 8 biscuits) refrigerated jumbo
   biscuits

3 tablespoons prepared pizza sauce

   Assorted pizza toppings such as pepperoni slices, cooked
      crumbled Italian sausage, sliced mushrooms and black
      olives

½ cup shredded pizza-blend or mozzarella cheese

1 egg yolk

1 teaspoon water

   Assorted food colorings

1. Preheat oven to 375°F. Press 4 biscuits into 4-inch rounds on
ungreased baking sheet. Spread center of each biscuit with about
2 teaspoons pizza sauce. Place 4 to 5 pepperoni slices or toppings of
your choice on each biscuit; top with 2 tablespoons cheese. Press
remaining 4 biscuits into 4-inch rounds and place over cheese; press
edges together to seal. Press design into top of each biscuit with
Halloween cookie cutter, being careful not to cut all the way through top
biscuit.

2. Combine egg yolk and water in small bowl. Divide yolk mixture into
several small bowls and tint each with food colorings to desired colors.
Decorate Halloween imprints with egg yolk paints. Bake 12 to
15 minutes or until biscuits are golden brown at edges.

Makes 4 servings

Note: This recipe tastes best when made with regular biscuits and not
butter-flavored biscuits.

• • • • • • • • • • • •

What do you get when a
monster steps on a house?

• • • • • • • • • • • •

Answer: Mushed rooms!

178

Dem Bones

1 package (6 ounces) sliced ham
¾ cup shredded Swiss cheese
½ cup mayonnaise
1 tablespoon sweet pickle relish
½ teaspoon mustard
¼ teaspoon black pepper
6 slices white bread

1. Place ham in bowl of food processor or blender; process until ground. Combine ham, cheese, mayonnaise, relish, mustard and pepper in small bowl until well blended.

2. Cut out 12 bone shapes from bread using 3½-inch bone-shaped cookie cutter or sharp knife. Spread half of "bones" with 2 tablespoons ham mixture; top with remaining "bones." *Makes 6 bone sandwiches*

Grilled Cheese Jack-O-Lanterns

3 tablespoons butter or margarine, softened
8 slices bread
4 slices Monterey Jack cheese
4 slices sharp Cheddar cheese

• Preheat oven to 350°F. Spread butter on one side of each bread slice. Place bread buttered-side-down on ungreased cookie sheet.

• Using small sharp hors d'oeuvre cutter or knife, cut out shapes from 4 bread slices to make jack-o-lantern faces. On remaining bread slices layer 1 slice Monterey Jack and 1 slice Cheddar.

• Bake 10 to 12 minutes or until cheese is melted. Remove from oven; place jack-o'-lantern bread slice on sandwiches and serve.

Makes 4 servings

180

Trick or Treat Ice Cream Sandwiches

½ cup margarine, softened

¾ cup granulated sugar

¾ cup packed light brown sugar

3 egg whites

1 teaspoon vanilla

2½ cups all-purpose flour

1½ teaspoons baking soda

1 teaspoon ground cinnamon

½ teaspoon salt

1 package (6 ounces) semisweet chocolate chips

1½ cups orange sherbet or any flavor nonfat frozen yogurt or ice cream, slightly softened

1. Preheat oven to 350°F. Spray baking sheets with nonstick cooking spray; set aside.

2. Beat margarine in large bowl until creamy. Add sugars; beat until fluffy. Blend in egg whites and vanilla. Combine flour, baking soda, cinnamon and salt in medium bowl. Add to margarine mixture; mix until well blended. Stir in chocolate chips.

3. Drop cookie dough by heaping teaspoonfuls onto prepared baking sheets, making 48 cookies. Bake until cookies are lightly browned, 10 to 12 minutes. Remove to wire racks to cool completely.

4. For each sandwich, place 1 tablespoon sherbet on flat side of 1 cookie; top with second cookie, flat side down. Press cookies together gently to even out sherbet layer. Repeat with remaining cookies and sherbet. Wrap tightly and store in freezer.

Makes 2 dozen sandwich cookies

Goblin Ice Cream Sandwiches: Prepare and freeze cookie sandwiches as directed. Just before serving, decorate 1 side of sandwich with Halloween candies or decorating gel to resemble goblin faces.

continued on page 184

Trick or Treats

Trick or Treat Ice Cream Sandwiches, continued

Colossal Cookie Sandwich: Prepare dough as directed. Substitute 2 lightly greased aluminum foil-lined 12-inch pizza pans for baking sheets. Prepare cookie dough as directed; divide evenly in half. Spread each half evenly onto bottom of prepared pizza pan to within ½ inch of outer edge. Bake until cookies are lightly browned, 10 to 15 minutes. Cool cookies in pans just until cookies begin to firm; slide off pans onto wire racks to cool completely. Spoon 1 quart (4 cups) frozen yogurt or ice cream onto flat side of 1 cookie. Top with remaining cookie, flat side down. Freeze until yogurt is firm, about 6 hours. Cut into wedges to serve. Makes 24 servings.

Sharing Cookies: Prepare dough as directed. Omit sherbet. Bake cookies on pizza pans as directed for Colossal Cookie Sandwich; cool completely. Serve cookies whole on large platters, allowing each person to break off their own piece. Makes 24 servings.

Individual Mashed Potato Ghosts

>   **5 cups mashed Idaho Potatoes**
>   **Waxed paper**
>   **½ cup small black olives**

1. Cut ghost shapes out of waxed paper to use as templates.

2. Place templates on serving dish or cookie sheet. Use rubber spatula to mold ½ to 1 cup potatoes into each ghost shape.

3. Slice olives to create circular shapes to be used for eyes and mouth.

Makes 4 to 6 servings

Note: To warm Mashed Potato Ghosts, microwave on HIGH 2 to 4 minutes on microwavable plate. If using oven, place potatoes on cookie sheet and re-heat at 350°F, loosely covered with foil, 7 to 8 minutes or until heated through.

Favorite recipe from **Idaho Potato Commission**

Magic Wands

Ingredients

1 cup semi-sweet chocolate chips

12 pretzel rods

3 ounces white chocolate baking bars or confectionery coating

Red and yellow food color

Assorted sprinkles

Supplies

Ribbon

1. Line baking sheet with waxed paper.

2. Melt semisweet chocolate in top of double boiler over hot, not boiling, water. Remove from heat. Dip pretzel rods into chocolate, spooning chocolate to coat about ¾ of each pretzel. Place on prepared baking sheet. Refrigerate until chocolate is firm.

3. Melt white chocolate in top of clean double boiler over hot, not boiling, water. Stir in food colors to make orange. Remove from heat. Dip coated pretzels quickly into colored white chocolate to coat about ¼ of each pretzel.

4. Place on baking sheet. Immediately top with sprinkles. Refrigerate until chocolate is firm.

5. Tie ends with ribbons.

Makes 12 wands

What do ghosts like to eat for lunch?

Answer: Spookghetti!

Creepy Crawler Punch

1 Creepy Crawler Ice Ring (recipe follows)
2 cups corn syrup
¼ cup water
6 cinnamon sticks
2 tablespoons whole cloves
½ teaspoon ground allspice
2 quarts cranberry juice cocktail
1½ quarts pineapple juice
1 quart orange juice
½ cup lemon juice
2 quarts ginger ale

1. The night or day before serving, prepare Creepy Crawler Ice Ring.

2. Stir together corn syrup and water in medium saucepan over medium-high heat. Add cinnamon sticks, cloves and allspice; stir gently. Bring to a boil and immediately reduce heat to a simmer; simmer 10 minutes.

3. Refrigerate, covered, until chilled. Remove cinnamon sticks and discard. Strain out cloves and discard.

4. In punch bowl, combine syrup mixture with juices and ginger ale. Unmold Creepy Crawler Ice Ring and add to punch bowl.

Makes 36 servings

Creepy Crawler Ice Ring

1 cup gummy worms or other creepy crawler candy
1 quart lemon-lime thirst quencher beverage

Arrange gummy worms in bottom of 5-cup ring mold; fill mold with thirst quencher beverage. Freeze until solid, 8 hours or overnight.

Creepy Cookie Cauldrons

1 package (18 ounces) refrigerated chocolate cookie dough*
All-purpose flour (optional)
1 bag (14 ounces) caramels, unwrapped
2 tablespoons milk
1 cup crisp rice cereal
¼ cup mini candy-coated chocolate pieces
Black licorice whips and small gummy insects, frogs or lizards

*If refrigerated chocolate cookie dough is unavailable, add ¼ cup unsweetened cocoa powder to refrigerated sugar cookie dough. Beat in large bowl until well blended.

1. Grease 36 (1¾-inch) mini muffin cups. Remove dough from wrapper according to package directions. Sprinkle dough with flour to minimize sticking, if necessary.

2. Cut dough into 36 equal pieces; roll into balls. Place 1 ball in bottom of each muffin cup. Press dough on bottoms and up sides of muffin cups; chill 15 minutes. Preheat oven to 350°F.

3. Bake 8 to 9 minutes. (Cookies will be puffy.) Remove from oven; gently press down center of each cookie. Return to oven 1 minute. Cool cookies in muffin cups 5 minutes. Remove to wire racks; cool completely.

4. Melt caramels and milk in small saucepan over low heat, stirring frequently until smooth. Stir in cereal. Spoon 1 heaping teaspoon caramel mixture into each cookie cup. Immediately sprinkle with mini chocolate pieces.

5. Cut licorice whips into 4½-inch lengths. For each cookie, make small slit in side; insert end of licorice strip. Repeat on other side of cookie to make cauldron handle. Decorate with gummy creatures as desired.

Makes 3 dozen cookies

Haunted Taco Tarts

    1 tablespoon vegetable oil

    ½ cup chopped onion

    ½ pound ground turkey

    1 clove garlic, minced

    ½ teaspoon dried oregano leaves

    ½ teaspoon chili powder

    ¼ teaspoon salt

    Egg Yolk Paint (recipe follows)

    1 package (15 ounces) refrigerated pie crusts

    1 egg white

    ½ cup chopped tomato

    ½ cup taco-flavored shredded cheese

• Heat oil in large skillet over medium heat. Add onion and cook until tender. Add turkey; cook until turkey is no longer pink, stirring occasionally. Stir in garlic, oregano, chili powder and salt; set aside. Preheat oven to 375°F. Lightly grease baking sheets. Prepare Egg Yolk Paint; set aside.

• On lightly floured surface, roll 1 pie crust to 14-inch diameter. Using 3-inch Halloween cookie cutters, cut out pairs of desired shapes. Repeat with second pie crust, rerolling dough if necessary. Place ½ of shapes on prepared baking sheets. Brush edges with egg white. Spoon about 1 tablespoon taco mixture onto each shape. Sprinkle with 1 teaspoon tomato and 1 teaspoon cheese. Top with remaining matching shapes; press edges to seal. Decorate with Egg Yolk Paint. Bake 10 to 12 minutes or until golden brown. *Makes 14 tarts*

Egg Yolk Paint

    4 egg yolks, divided

    4 teaspoons water, divided

    Red, yellow, blue and green liquid food colors

Place 1 egg yolk in each of 4 small bowls. Add 1 teaspoon water and few drops different food color to each; beat lightly.

Haunted Taco Tarts

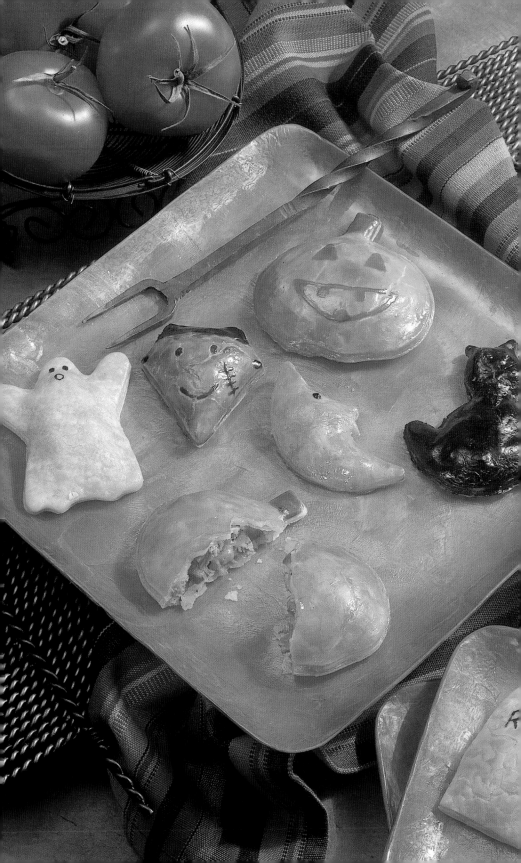

Witches' Snack Hats

1 package (18 ounces) refrigerated sugar cookie dough

¼ cup unsweetened cocoa powder

1½ cups semisweet chocolate chips, divided

16 sugar ice cream cones

⅓ cup butter

3 cups dry cereal (mixture of puffed corn, bite-sized wheat and toasted oat cereal)

½ cup roasted pumpkin seeds

½ cup chopped dried cherries or raisins

1⅓ cups powdered sugar

Assorted colored sugars and decors

1. Preheat oven to 350°F. Grease cookie sheets; set aside. Remove dough from wrapper according to package directions. Combine dough and cocoa powder in large bowl; mix until well blended. Evenly divide dough into 16 pieces; shape into balls. Flatten each ball onto prepared cookie sheet into 3½- to 4-inch circle. Bake 6 to 8 minutes or until set. Cool on cookie sheets 5 minutes; transfer to wire racks to cool completely.

2. Line large tray with waxed paper. Place 1 cup chocolate chips in small microwavable bowl. Microwave at HIGH 1 to 1½ minutes or until melted, stirring at 30-second intervals. Coat sugar cones with chocolate using clean pastry brush. Stand up on prepared tray; let set.

3. Place remaining ½ cup chocolate chips and butter in small microwavable bowl. Microwave at HIGH 1 to 1½ minutes or until melted, stirring at 30-second intervals. Stir mixture to blend well. Place cereal, pumpkin seeds and cherries in large bowl. Pour chocolate mixture over cereal mixture and stir until thoroughly coated. Sprinkle mixture with powdered sugar, ⅓ cup at a time, carefully folding and mixing until thoroughly coated.

continued on page 194

Witches' Snack Hats, continued

4. Fill cone with snack mix. Brush cone edge with melted chocolate; attach to center of cookie and let set. Repeat with remaining cones, snack mix and cookies. Decorate hats as desired with melted chocolate, colored sugars and decors. *Makes 16 servings*

Hint: To use these hats as place cards, simply write each guest's name on the hat with melted white chocolate, frosting or decorating gel.

Bat & Spook Pizzas

> 4 (6-inch) Italian bread shells
> ⅔ cup pizza or spaghetti sauce
> 1 package (3½ ounces) pepperoni slices
> 4 slices (1 ounce each) mozzarella cheese

1. Preheat oven to 375°F. Place bread shells on ungreased baking sheet.

2. Spread pizza sauce evenly on bread shells; top evenly with pepperoni slices.

3. Cut out ghost and bat shapes from cheese slices with cookie cutters; place on pizza sauce.

4. Bake 10 to 12 minutes or until cheese is melted.

Makes 4 servings

Pumpkin Pizzas: Spread bread shells with pizza sauce as directed. Substitute process American cheese slices for mozzarella; cut into triangles. Place cheese triangles on pizza sauce to make jack-o-lantern faces. Omit pepperoni slices. Add ¼ cup broccoli florets for eyes and 2 cherry tomatoes, halved, for noses. Bake as directed.

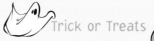

Monster Claws

2 tablespoons flour

1 tablespoon plus 2 teaspoons cajun seasoning, divided

1 pound boneless skinless chicken breasts, cut lengthwise into ¾-inch strips

1½ cups cornflake crumbs

2 tablespoons chopped green onion

3 eggs, lightly beaten

1 red, yellow or orange bell pepper, cut into triangles

Barbecue sauce

- Preheat oven to 350°F. Lightly grease baking sheets. Place flour and 2 teaspoons cajun seasoning in large resealable plastic food storage bag. Add chicken and seal. Shake bag to coat chicken.

- Combine cornflake crumbs, green onion and remaining 1 tablespoon cajun seasoning in large shallow bowl; mix well. Place eggs in shallow bowl.

- Dip each chicken strip into eggs and then into crumb mixture. Place coated chicken strips on prepared baking sheet.

- Bake chicken strips 8 to 10 minutes or until chicken is no longer pink in center.

- When chicken is cool enough to handle, make ½-inch slit in thinner end. Place bell pepper triangle into slit to form claw nail. Serve claws with barbecue sauce for dipping. *Makes about 30 strips*

● ● ● ● ● ● ● ● ● ● ● ●

What is a ghost's favorite dessert?

● ● ● ● ● ● ● ● ● ● ● ●

Answer: Booberry pie!

Cookie Pizza

1 (18-ounce) package refrigerated sugar cookie dough

2 cups (12 ounces) semi-sweet chocolate chips

1 (14-ounce) can **EAGLE® BRAND** Sweetened Condensed
Milk (**NOT** evaporated milk)

2 cups candy-coated milk chocolate candies

2 cups miniature marshmallows

½ cup peanuts

1. Preheat oven to 375°F. Press cookie dough into 2 ungreased 12-inch pizza pans. Bake 10 minutes or until golden. Remove from oven.

2. In medium-sized saucepan, melt chips with Eagle Brand. Spread over crusts. Sprinkle with milk chocolate candies, marshmallows and peanuts.

3. Bake 4 minutes or until marshmallows are lightly toasted. Cool. Cut into wedges. *Makes 2 pizzas (24 servings)*

Prep Time: 15 minutes
Bake Time: 14 minutes

• • • • • • • • • • • •

**What did the baby corn
say to the mommy corn?**

• • • • • • • • • • • •

Answer: Where's pop corn?

Magical Marshmallow Carpets

1 package (8-serving size) *or* 2 packages (4-serving size each)
    JELL-O® Brand Gelatin, any flavor

1 cup warm water

3 cups JET-PUFFED® Miniature Marshmallows *or*
    12 JET-PUFFED® Marshmallows

LIGHTLY GREASE 13×9-inch baking pan with no stick cooking spray.

STIR gelatin and water in medium microwavable bowl. Microwave on
HIGH 2½ minutes; stir until dissolved.

STIR in marshmallows. Microwave on HIGH 2 minutes or until
marshmallows are partially melted. Stir mixture slowly until
marshmallows are completely melted. Pour mixture into pan.

REFRIGERATE 1 hour or until set. Cut gelatin into 2¼×4¼-inch
rectangles. With marshmallow layer on top, cut small slits on each side of
the rectangles to form "carpet fringes." Garnish each "carpet" with
multicolored sprinkles, if desired.   *Makes 16 pieces*

Variation: To make JELL-O® Marshmallow JIGGLERS®, do not cut into
rectangles. Cut out shapes with 1-inch metal cookie cutters. For 2-color
JIGGLERS®, prepare recipe as directed above. After refrigerating, repeat
recipe in same pan with another gelatin flavor. Cut out shapes.

Prep Time: 10 minutes plus refrigerating

198

Chocolate-Caramel S'Mores

12 chocolate wafer cookies or chocolate graham cracker squares
2 tablespoons fat-free caramel topping
6 large marshmallows

1. Prepare coals for grilling. Place 6 wafer cookies top-down on plate. Spread 1 teaspoon caramel topping in center of each wafer to within about ¼ inch of edge.

2. Spear 1 to 2 marshmallows onto long wood-handled skewer.* Hold several inches above coals 3 to 5 minutes or until marshmallows are golden and very soft, turning slowly. Push 1 marshmallow off into center of caramel. Top with plain wafer. Repeat with remaining marshmallows and wafers.   *Makes 6 servings*

*If wood-handled skewers are unavailable, use oven mitt to protect hand from heat.

Note: S'mores, a favorite campfire treat, got their name because everyone who tasted them wanted "some more." In the unlikely event of leftover S'mores, they can be reheated in the microwave at HIGH 15 to 30 seconds.

Funny Face Cookies

4 large cookies (about 4 inches in diameter)
½ cup thawed COOL WHIP® Whipped Topping
Assorted candies and sprinkles
BAKER'S® Semi-Sweet Real Chocolate Chunks
Toasted BAKER'S ANGEL FLAKE® Coconut

SPREAD each cookie with about 2 tablespoons of the whipped topping.

DECORATE with candies, sprinkles, chunks and coconut to resemble faces. Serve immediately.   *Makes 4 servings*

200

Sunflower Cookies in Flowerpots

   1 recipe **Butter Cookie** dough (recipe page 204)
   1 container (16 ounces) vanilla frosting
     Yellow food color
     Powdered sugar
   1 gallon ice cream (any flavor), softened
     Brown decorating icing
  24 chocolate sandwich cookies, crushed
   1 cup shredded coconut, tinted green

Supplies

  12 (6-inch) lollipop sticks
   6 plastic drinking straws
  12 (6½-ounce) paper cups
     Pastry bag and small writing tip
  12 new (3¼-inch-diameter) ceramic flowerpots, about
        3½ inches tall

1. Prepare Butter Cookie Dough.

2. Preheat oven to 350°F. Grease cookie sheets. Roll dough on lightly floured surface to ⅛-inch thickness. Cut out dough with 3-inch flower-shaped cookie cutters; place on prepared cookie sheets.

3. Bake 8 to 10 minutes or until edges are lightly browned. Remove to wire racks; cool completely.

4. Tint vanilla frosting with yellow food color. Reserve ⅔ cup yellow frosting. Cover remaining yellow frosting; set aside. Blend enough additional powdered sugar into reserved yellow frosting to make a very thick frosting. Use about 1 tablespoon thickened frosting to attach lollipop stick to back of each cookie. Set aside to allow frosting to dry completely.

continued on page 204

Sunflower Cookies in Flowerpots, continued

5. Cut straws crosswise in half. Hold 1 straw upright in center of each paper cup; pack ice cream around straw, completely filling each cup with ice cream. (Be sure straw sticks up out of ice cream.) Freeze until ice cream is hardened, 3 to 4 hours.

6. Frost front side of each cookie as desired with remaining yellow frosting. Spoon brown icing into pastry bag fitted with writing tip; decorate cookies as shown in photo.

7. To serve, clip off straw to make even with ice cream. Place ice cream-filled cups in flowerpots. Insert lollipop stick, with cookie attached, into opening in each straw to stand cookie upright in flowerpot. Sprinkle ice cream with cookie crumbs to resemble dirt; sprinkle with green coconut to resemble grass.   *Makes 12 servings*

Note: To tint coconut, dilute a few drops of food color with ½ teaspoon water in a large plastic bag. Add 1 to 1⅓ cups flaked coconut. Close the bag and shake well until the coconut is evenly coated. If a deeper color is desired, add more diluted food color and shake again.

Butter Cookie Dough

  ¾ **cup butter, softened**
  ¼ **cup granulated sugar**
  ¼ **cup packed light brown sugar**
   1 **egg yolk**
1¾ **cups all-purpose flour**
  ¾ **teaspoon baking powder**
  ⅛ **teaspoon salt**

1. Combine butter, granulated sugar, brown sugar and egg yolk in medium bowl. Add flour, baking powder and salt; mix well.

2. Cover; refrigerate about 4 hours or until firm.

Peanut Butter Bears

2 cups quick-cooking rolled oats
2 cups all-purpose flour
I tablespoon baking powder
I cup granulated sugar
¾ cup butter, softened
½ cup creamy peanut butter
½ cup packed brown sugar
½ cup cholesterol-free egg substitute
I teaspoon vanilla
3 tablespoons miniature chocolate chips

1. Stir together rolled oats, flour and baking powder; set aside.

2. Beat granulated sugar, butter, peanut butter and brown sugar in large mixer bowl with mixer at medium-high speed until creamed. Add egg substitute and vanilla; beat until light and fluffy. Add rolled oat mixture. Beat on low speed until combined. Cover and refrigerate I to 2 hours or until easy to handle.

3. Preheat oven to 375°F.

4. For each bear, shape one I-inch ball for body and one ¾-inch ball for head. Place body and head together on baking sheet; flatten slightly. Make 7 small balls for ears, arms, legs and mouth. Place on bear body and head. Place 2 chocolate chips on each head for eyes; place I chocolate chip on each body for belly-button.

5. Bake 9 to 11 minutes or until light brown. Cool I minute on cookie sheet. Remove to wire racks; cool completely.

Makes 4 dozen cookies

Dessert Nachos

3 (6- to 7-inch) flour tortillas
Nonstick cooking spray
1 tablespoon sugar
⅛ teaspoon ground cinnamon
Dash ground allspice
1 (6- or 8-ounce) container fat-free sugar-free vanilla yogurt
1 teaspoon grated orange peel
1½ cups strawberries
½ cup blueberries
4 teaspoons miniature semisweet chocolate chips

1. Preheat oven to 375°F.

2. Cut each flour tortilla into 8 wedges. Place on ungreased baking sheet. Generously spray tortilla wedges with cooking spray. Stir together sugar, cinnamon and allspice. Sprinkle over tortilla wedges. Bake 7 to 9 minutes or until lightly browned; cool completely.

3. Meanwhile, stir together yogurt and orange peel. Stem strawberries; cut lengthwise into fourths.

4. Place 6 tortilla wedges on each of 4 small plates. Top with strawberries and blueberries. Drizzle yogurt mixture on top. Sprinkle with chocolate chips. Serve immediately.   *Makes 4 servings*

"Everything but the Kitchen Sink" Bar Cookies

1 package (18 ounces) refrigerated chocolate chip cookie dough
1 jar (7 ounces) marshmallow creme
½ cup creamy peanut butter
1½ cups toasted corn cereal
½ cup miniature candy-coated chocolate pieces

1. Preheat oven to 350°F. Grease 13×9-inch baking pan. Remove dough from wrapper according to package directions.

2. Press dough into prepared baking pan. Bake 13 minutes.

3. Remove baking pan from oven. Drop teaspoonfuls of marshmallow creme and peanut butter over hot cookie base.

4. Bake 1 minute. Carefully spread marshmallow creme and peanut butter over cookie base.

5. Sprinkle cereal and chocolate pieces over melted marshmallow and peanut butter mixture.

6. Bake 7 minutes. Cool completely on wire rack. Cut into 2-inch bars.

Makes 3 dozen bars

Super Suggestion!

Experiment with this recipe using your favorite candies. Try substituting peanut butter chips in place of chocolate pieces.

Mice Creams

I pint vanilla ice cream

I (4-ounce) package **READY CRUST®** Mini-Graham Cracker Pie Crusts

Ears—12 **KEEBLER®** Grasshopper® cookies

Tails—3 chocolate twigs, broken in half *or* 6 (3-inch) pieces black shoestring licorice

Eyes and noses—18 brown candy-coated chocolate candies

Whiskers—2 teaspoons chocolate sprinkles

Place 1 scoop vanilla ice cream into each crust. Press cookie ears and tails into ice cream. Press eyes, noses and whiskers in place. Serve immediately. Do not refreeze. *Makes 6 servings*

Prep Time: 15 minutes

Polar Bear Banana Bites

1 medium banana, cut into 6 equal-size pieces

¼ cup creamy peanut butter*

3 tablespoons fat-free (skim) milk

¼ cup miniature-size marshmallows

2 tablespoons unsalted dry-roasted peanuts, chopped

1 tablespoon chocolate-flavored decorator sprinkles

Soy butter or almond butter can be used in place of peanut butter.

1. Insert wooden pick into each banana piece. Place on tray lined with waxed paper.

2. Whisk together peanut butter and milk. Combine marshmallows, peanuts and chocolate sprinkles in shallow dish. Dip each banana piece in peanut butter mixture, draining off excess. Roll in peanut mixture. Place on tray; let stand until set. *Makes 3 servings*

Frozen Berry Ice Cream

8 ounces frozen unsweetened strawberries, partially thawed

8 ounces frozen unsweetened peaches, partially thawed

4 ounces frozen unsweetened blueberries, partially thawed

6 packets sugar substitute

2 teaspoons vanilla

2 cups no-sugar-added light vanilla ice cream

16 blueberries

4 small strawberries, halved

8 peach slices

1. In food processor, combine frozen strawberries, peaches, blueberries, sugar substitute and vanilla. Process until coarsely chopped.

2. Add ice cream; process until well blended.

3. Serve immediately for semi-soft texture or freeze until needed and allow to stand 10 minutes to soften slightly. Garnish each serving with 2 blueberries for "eyes," 1 strawberry half for "nose" and 1 peach slice for "smile."   *Makes 8 servings ($\frac{1}{2}$ cup each)*

Cookies and Creme Snacks

1 cup chocolate sandwich cookie crumbs *or* chocolate wafer cookie crumbs

1 tub (8 ounces) COOL WHIP® Whipped Topping, thawed

STIR cookie crumbs into whipped topping. Spoon into snack cups or flat-bottom ice cream cones.

REFRIGERATE or freeze until ready to serve.

Makes 6 to 8 servings

Prep Time: 5 minutes

Bamboozlers

1 cup all-purpose flour

¾ cup packed light brown sugar

¼ cup unsweetened cocoa powder

1 egg

2 egg whites

5 tablespoons margarine, melted

¼ cup fat-free (skim) milk

¼ cup honey

1 teaspoon vanilla

2 tablespoons semisweet chocolate chips

2 tablespoons coarsely chopped walnuts

Powdered sugar (optional)

1. Preheat oven to 350°F. Grease and flour 8-inch square baking pan; set aside.

2. Combine flour, brown sugar and cocoa in medium bowl. Blend together egg, egg whites, margarine, milk, honey and vanilla in medium bowl. Add to flour mixture; mix well. Pour into prepared baking pan; sprinkle with chocolate chips and walnuts.

3. Bake brownies until they spring back when lightly touched in center, about 30 minutes. Cool completely in pan on wire rack. Sprinkle with powdered sugar just before serving.   *Makes 1 dozen brownies*

Peanutters: Substitute peanut butter chips for chocolate chips and peanuts for walnuts.

Butterscotch Babies: Substitute butterscotch chips for chocolate chips and pecans for walnuts.

Brownie Sundaes: Serve brownies on dessert plates. Top each brownie with a scoop of vanilla nonfat frozen yogurt and 2 tablespoons nonfat chocolate or caramel sauce.

Puzzle Cookie

¾ cup shortening
½ cup packed light brown sugar
6 tablespoons dark molasses
2 egg whites
¾ teaspoon vanilla
2¼ cups all-purpose flour
2 teaspoons ground cinnamon
¾ teaspoon baking soda
¾ teaspoon salt
¾ teaspoon ground ginger
¼ teaspoon plus ⅛ teaspoon baking powder
Assorted colored frostings, colored sugars, colored decorator gels and assorted small candies

1. Beat shortening, brown sugar, molasses, egg whites and vanilla in large bowl at high speed of electric mixer until smooth.

2. Combine flour, cinnamon, baking soda, salt, ginger and baking powder in medium bowl. Add to shortening mixture; mix well. Shape dough into flat rectangle. Wrap in plastic wrap and refrigerate about 8 hours or until firm.

3. Preheat oven to 350°F. Grease 15½×10½-inch jelly-roll pan.

4. Sprinkle dough with additional flour. Place dough in center of prepared pan and roll evenly to within ½ inch of edge of pan. Cut shapes into dough using cookie cutters or free-hand, using sharp knife, allowing at least 1 inch between each shape. Cut through dough, but do not remove shapes.

5. Bake 12 minutes or until edges begin to brown lightly. Remove from oven and retrace shapes with knife. Return to oven 5 to 6 minutes. Cool in pan 5 minutes. Carefully remove shapes to wire racks; cool completely.

6. Decorate shapes with frostings, sugars, decorator gels and small candies. Leave puzzle frame in pan. Decorate with frostings, colored sugars and gels to represent sky, clouds, grass and water, if desired. Return shapes to their respective openings to complete puzzle.

Makes 1 puzzle cookie

Ice Cream Cone Cakes

1 package (18¼ ounces) devil's food cake mix plus ingredients to prepare mix

⅓ cup sour cream

1 package (2⅝ ounces) flat-bottomed ice cream cones (about 18 cones)

1¼ cups nonfat frozen yogurt (any flavor)

Cake decorations or chocolate sprinkles

1. Preheat oven to 350°F. Grease and flour 8- or 9-inch round cake pan; set aside.

2. Prepare cake mix according to package directions, substituting sour cream for ⅓ cup of water and decreasing oil to ¼ cup.

3. Spoon ½ of batter (about 2⅓ cups) evenly into ice cream cones, using about 2 tablespoons batter for each. Pour remaining batter into prepared cake pan.

4. Stand cones on cookie sheet. Bake cones and cake layer until toothpick inserted into center of cake comes out clean, about 20 minutes for cones and about 35 minutes for cake layer. Cool on wire racks, removing cake from pan after 10 minutes. Reserve or freeze cake layer for another use.

5. Top each filled cone with ¼ scoop of frozen yogurt just before serving. Sprinkle with decorations as desired. Serve immediately.

Makes 18 servings

Acknowledgments

The publisher would like to thank the companies and organizations listed below for the use of their recipes and photographs in this publication.

California Tree Fruit Agreement

ConAgra Foods®

Dole Food Company, Inc.

Eagle Brand®

Hebrew National®

Hershey Foods Corporation

Hillshire Farm®

Idaho Potato Commission

JOLLY TIME® Pop Corn

Keebler® Company

Kraft Foods Holdings

© Mars, Incorporated 2004

Mott's® is a registered trademark of Mott's, Inc.

National Cherry Growers & Industries Foundation

National Honey Board

Newman's Own, Inc.®

Reckitt Benckiser Inc.

The J.M. Smucker Company

StarKist® Seafood Company

Sun•Maid® Growers of California

Index

Index

METRIC CONVERSION CHART

VOLUME MEASUREMENTS (dry)

$^1/_8$ teaspoon = 0.5 mL
$^1/_4$ teaspoon = 1 mL
$^1/_2$ teaspoon = 2 mL
$^3/_4$ teaspoon = 4 mL
1 teaspoon = 5 mL
1 tablespoon = 15 mL
2 tablespoons = 30 mL
$^1/_4$ cup = 60 mL
$^1/_3$ cup = 75 mL
$^1/_2$ cup = 125 mL
$^2/_3$ cup = 150 mL
$^3/_4$ cup = 175 mL
1 cup = 250 mL
2 cups = 1 pint = 500 mL
3 cups = 750 mL
4 cups = 1 quart = 1 L

VOLUME MEASUREMENTS (fluid)

1 fluid ounce (2 tablespoons) = 30 mL
4 fluid ounces ($^1/_2$ cup) = 125 mL
8 fluid ounces (1 cup) = 250 mL
12 fluid ounces (1$^1/_2$ cups) = 375 mL
16 fluid ounces (2 cups) = 500 mL

WEIGHTS (mass)

$^1/_2$ ounce = 15 g
1 ounce = 30 g
3 ounces = 90 g
4 ounces = 120 g
8 ounces = 225 g
10 ounces = 285 g
12 ounces = 360 g
16 ounces = 1 pound = 450 g

DIMENSIONS

$^1/_{16}$ inch = 2 mm
$^1/_8$ inch = 3 mm
$^1/_4$ inch = 6 mm
$^1/_2$ inch = 1.5 cm
$^3/_4$ inch = 2 cm
1 inch = 2.5 cm

OVEN TEMPERATURES

250°F = 120°C
275°F = 140°C
300°F = 150°C
325°F = 160°C
350°F = 180°C
375°F = 190°C
400°F = 200°C
425°F = 220°C
450°F = 230°C

BAKING PAN SIZES

Utensil	Size in Inches/Quarts	Metric Volume	Size in Centimeters
Baking or Cake Pan (square or rectangular)	8×8×2	2 L	20×20×5
	9×9×2	2.5 L	23×23×5
	12×8×2	3 L	30×20×5
	13×9×2	3.5 L	33×23×5
Loaf Pan	8×4×3	1.5 L	20×10×7
	9×5×3	2 L	23×13×7
Round Layer Cake Pan	8×1½	1.2 L	20×4
	9×1½	1.5 L	23×4
Pie Plate	8×1¼	750 mL	20×3
	9×1¼	1 L	23×3
Baking Dish or Casserole	1 quart	1 L	—
	1½ quart	1.5 L	—
	2 quart	2 L	—